CORPORATE TAKEOVERS
AND THE PUBLIC INTEREST

Corporate Takeovers and the Public Interest

Report of an Inquiry conducted for
the Joseph Rowntree Foundation by
THE DAVID HUME INSTITUTE

The Report was prepared by Sir Alan Peacock, Chairman
of the Inquiry and Graham Bannock, Research Director.
'Jock' Snaith, Secretary of the Inquiry, prepared the
Summary of Evidence.

ABERDEEN UNIVERSITY PRESS
Member of the Maxwell Macmillan Pergammon Publishing Corporation

First Published 1991
Aberdeen University Press
© The David Hume Institute 1991

British Library Cataloguing in Publication Data

A catalogue record for this book
is available from the British Library.

ISBN 0-08-041206-8

Printed in Great Britain
by BPCC-AUP Aberdeen Ltd

Contents

PART II ANALYSIS

PART III POLICY

Figures and Tables

Foreword

The following Report is the result of an Inquiry into Corporate Takeovers in the United Kingdom undertaken by The David Hume Institute for the Joseph Rowntree Foundation. The terms of reference of the Inquiry were:

i) to review the evidence of the present and future dimensions of takeover activity and the likely results;
ii) to examine the market, legislative and supervisory mechanisms through which takeover activity is conducted;
iii) to assess the consequences of takeovers in relation to economic efficiency and the public interest, having regard to regional and local factors;
iv) in the light of (i) to (iii), to consider the present methods of controlling takeover activity and to make recommendations.

The Institute was also required to conduct a case study into the Rowntree/Nestlé takeover.

The progress of the Inquiry was monitored by a Steering Committee appointed by the Foundation and its members are as follows.

Graham Bannock, Managing Director of the economic consultancy Graham Bannock and Partners Ltd
Sir Donald Barron, Chairman of the Joseph Rowntree Foundation
Sir Adrian Cadbury, a Director of the Bank of England; Chairman of Cadbury Schweppes plc 1975–89
Jonathan Charkham, Adviser to the Governors of the Bank of England
Professor Richard Dale, Coopers Deloitte Professor of International Banking at the University of Southampton
Professor Robert Jack, Senior Partner, McGrigor Donald, Solicitors and Professor of Mercantile Law, University of Glasgow
Jeffrey Knight, Special Adviser to the Federation of Stock Exchanges in EC Countries; Chief Executive, Stock Exchange 1982–89
Professor Sir Alan Peacock, Executive Director, The David Hume Institute 1985–90
Professor John C. Shaw, Deputy Governor, Bank of Scotland
H.L. Snaith, Secretary, The David Hume Institute 1985–90, Registrar Birkbeck College, University of London 1966–83

I was appointed Chairman of the Committee, with Mr. Graham Bannock as Research Director and Mr. H. L. Snaith as Secretary. Mr. Bannock and I were responsible for the drafting of the main body of the Report and Mr. Snaith helped with the editing of the Report and prepared the Summary of the Research Reports and Evidence which is contained in the Appendix.

The Introduction to this Report, which follows, describes the analytical methods used in its preparation, but a few words on the procedure followed by the Inquiry may be helpful to the reader. The function of the Committee may be of particular interest. The Inquiry began in October 1989 and the Steering Committee met on 5th January 1990 in order to approve the research programme and the list of organisations whom the Institute might approach to give evidence. The Committee agreed that research reports and evidence should be published as soon as available, subject to editing, and 16 Hume Occasional Papers (called HOPs for short) contain research findings and submissions. In subsequent meetings of the Committee these reports and evidence were discussed and advice sought on further research reports and submissions that might be obtained. Draft chapters began appearing in the late Spring of 1990 and were fully discussed with a view to amendment and enlargement. The first full draft of the Report was available in early March 1991 and was discussed at length at an extended meeting on 13/14th March held at the Foundation's York headquarters. The final report, embodying suggested amendments, was delivered to the Aberdeen University Press on 5th April 1991.

I should like to express my profound gratitude to the members of the Steering Committee for sparing the time and taking the trouble to put their very considerable knowledge and expertise at the disposal of the Inquiry. It is inconceivable that the Report could have been written without their help and guidance. They have approved the general stance taken in the Report, but are in no way responsible for the detailed analysis and the particular recommendations which Graham Bannock and I have put forward. I must also express my deep appreciation of the financial support offered by the Foundation, as well as thanking them warmly for the advice of its officials on such matters as arrangement of meetings, press conferences and press coverage.

It is a pleasure to acknowledge the interest shown and tangible help offered by many individuals, by professional and business organisations, and by Government agencies and Departments. A full list of them is given in the Appendix.

It would have been impossible to have issued the reports and evidence at great speed without the full co-operation of Mr. E. Dalgleish of Pace Print (Edinburgh) which is gratefully acknowledged.

The secretarial and administrative help given by the staff of Graham Bannock and Partners has been magnificent as has that of Ms. Kathy Mountain, personal assistant to the Executive Director of The David Hume Institute.

Finally, I must confess to having placed intolerable burdens on two old friends and colleagues, Graham and 'Jock', in our endeavours to produce this Report within the required time limits. I apologise to them both, but believe that they have quite enjoyed yet another venture punctuated by more than the usual number of difficulties and uncertainties!

Alan Peacock
March 1991

1 Introduction

I Background

Merger activity, and especially contested takeover bids, have aroused concern and controversy in the UK – and indeed in other countries – on many occasions during the past 40 years. This concern has been most widespread at times when merger activity, which fluctuates in cycles, has peaked, as in 1965, 1972 and more recently in 1988–89.

Mergers, in fact, raise a number of important questions to which satisfactory answers are not easy to find. Amongst those of particular contemporary interest are the following.

i) What is the extent of merger activity?

ii) How important are contested bids in the merger process?

iii) What are the factors favouring takeovers?

iv) Is takeover activity an essential element in promoting economic performance?

v) Do takeovers affect the distribution of economic power between national economies and regional economies?

vi) Are particular issues raised by takeover activity concerning the ethics of business behaviour?

vii) Is the stance of the Government towards takeover activity a satisfactory one?

viii) What changes, if any, should be made in the Government's policies towards takeovers?

The Trustees of the Joseph Rowntree Foundation considered that these and related questions needed thorough investigation with a view to formulating recommendations for public policy towards takeovers. This Report is the result of such an investigation and offers some far-reaching recommendations to policy makers.

II Procedure

No doubt as a result of the contemporary interest in and concern about takeovers, there is a vast array of statistical information, economic analysis, policy recommendations and government statements covering the subject. This presents both an opportunity and a challenge to the authors of this Report. The opportunity lies in being able to draw upon a substantial archive of material which makes it possible to speed up the process of Inquiry. If nothing else, this Report performs the function of collating this material with copious reference to and commentary on its findings, as will be evident from the extensive bibliography. It would not have been possible to have finished the Inquiry within 18 months without having access to the extensive work of other investigators to whom we are greatly indebted.

The challenge consists in how to differentiate our product from that of previous studies. An important part of our work, as mentioned in the Preface, was to carry out a case study of the takeover of Rowntree by Nestlé. This has been done and published as a separate paper (see Davis and Bannock, HOP 30). However, although this contested acquisition raises most of the important questions listed earlier, it took place in 1988 and is too recent to draw final conclusions which could not, in any event, rest on one case, however important. We were of a mind in the earlier stages of the investigation simply to base our findings on existing research and to rely on our perceptions of the value of that research for the derivation of conclusions and policy recommendations. As we have already indicated, becoming *au fait* with existing data and analyses is quite a formidable task. We soon found out that there are considerable gaps in knowledge of the takeover process and we developed misgivings about the way in which economic analysis has been employed to appraise the effects of takeover activity. Furthermore, policy recommendations on the control of takeover activity cover a very narrow range of measures mainly related to the Government's competition policy. Meeting the challenge of product differentiation required us to initiate research of our own, to seek evidence on less well known aspects of takeovers and to develop our own analytical and policy framework. The reader must judge how successful we may have been in fulfilling this self-imposed task, but some preliminary indication of how we set about it may assist him or her.

The first part of the Report offers an overview of the takeover phenomenon. We found that there are major gaps in our information on the extent of takeover within the UK and on the comparative importance of takeover in industrial countries, considered both in cross-section and historical terms. One of us (Graham Bannock) spent a considerable period in the initial stages of the Inquiry on an attempt to fill these gaps (See Bannock, HOP 15). It also became clear that the importance of institutional investors in the supply of corporate finance, while widely recognised, was not matched by knowledge of their methods of appraisal of companies 'in play' and of their attitudes to takeovers. The Inquiry therefore commissioned Professor and Mrs. Morgan to conduct an independent survey of institutional investors and their results, along with those of Bannock (op.cit.) represent a substantial addition to our knowledge of the workings of the stock market and about whether or not this market is able to discriminate effectively between mergers that are and those that are not 'in the public interest' (See Morgan and Morgan, HOPs 24 and 25).

The second part of the Report is built round an analysis of the relation between corporate takeovers and economic performance. There is a mammoth literature, much of it emanating from the USA, on this subject which is centred on the efficient market hypothesis. An 'efficient capital market' is defined as one which operates to select the most profitable investment opportunities. In applying the hypothesis to the market for corporate control, it is contended that only those mergers and takeovers will succeed which will improve the profitability of the companies involved. We have found it useful to take these propositions as the point of departure for close analysis of the relation between takeovers and various alternative ways of measuring economic performance. In particular, helped by commissioned reports by Gavin Reid (HOP 22) and Professor and Mrs. Morgan (op.cit.) we have considered very carefully the assumption underlying the efficient market hypothesis, drawing particular attention to the attenuated link between shareholders and the assets to which they lay claim which makes the capital market a battleground, in the UK at least, between conflicting interests – shareholders, institutions which invest their capital, managers of firms and consumers. Our approach also made it necessary to consider the tests used in linking takeovers to economic performance in a particular light and to adopt a critical stance towards accounting studies of profitability which have been used in the assessment of merger performance. We believe that our approach, backed by both the research reports and evidence submitted, offers a firmer basis for a judgment on the economic effects of takeovers than that presented in Government documents.

The third part of the Report turns to questions of policy. Again, there is a wealth of documents recording both the evolution of government policies and criticising them, and we have familiarised ourselves with a fair proportion of them. We could have contented ourselves with using these as the only necessary source material, but we took advantage of a unique opportunity to supplement them. The interest shown by Government departments and agencies extended to the presentation of evidence on their present policy stance and we are very grateful to the Department of Trade and Industry, the Office of Fair Trading and the Scottish Office for their submissions. We also took advantage of the offer of advice and guidance from the Inland Revenue on tax policy and takeovers and from the European Commission through the good offices of Sir Leon Brittan, the Commissioner for Competition Policy. Given the important role of the Takeover Panel in the UK we commissioned a review of the activities (see Manser, HOP 21) and a further study of the increasingly important role of the European Commission in takeover regulation (see Pringle, HOP 29).

The final element in our attempt to differentiate our analytical product lies in our approach to the appraisal of the Government's policies. We try to set out a methodology of appraisal which distinguishes between criticisms which emanate from disagreements about the Government's aims and those which emanate from doubts about the consistency of the Government's policies with its own stated aims. We pay some attention to the wider aims of policy which have been thrown into discussion by those concerned about the effects of takeovers on the regional economies of the UK and about standards of business behaviour but share the Government's doubts about the appropriateness of basing any reform of business policy solely on further controls on takeovers. However, our main contention is that the Government's policy is based on the dubious proposition that mergers and takeovers are almost a necessary condition for the health of the British economy. We contend that takeovers frequently represent distortions in the market which are at variance with the Government's own fundamental policy of improving competitiveness.

III Results

Our recommendations for policy changes are set out in a final chapter. Again we are faced with a wealth of such recommendations which come to the fore every time that a prominent contested takeover hits the headlines. Some of them are based on serious study of the market for corporate control and it would only be right to look at these.

The essence of our own approach to reform is to look again at the nature of the competitive process. While accepting the Government's view that the clue to our economic performance, upon which our social and cultural development depends, lies in competitiveness, we consider that the concept of competition which governs policy is too narrowly conceived and is not consistently applied. If competition is perceived as a dynamic process in which there is freedom of entry into all sectors of economic activity, and process and product innovations have a better chance of success, then lowering barriers to entry becomes the keystone of policy. Such an approach has quite profound implications for the operation of the capital market, for tax policies and for corporate governance. In particular, it points towards the removal of distortions in favour of takeovers.

PART I: DESCRIPTIVE

1 The Aims and Strategies of Takeovers

I Definition

A *takeover* is the acquisition of the whole of the equity share capital of one company by another. Strictly speaking, a takeover is distinct from the acquisition of a minority stake by one company in another, even if that stake is sufficient to give *de facto* control, though in practice the practical consequences may be little different. (The City Code requires that once a company has acquired 30 per cent of the voting rights of a company, it must make an offer for the remainder.)

In this report we use the terms *takeover*, *acquisition* and *merger* as synonyms. 'Merger' is sometimes used to refer to the pooling of the share capital of two companies of roughly equal size, whether or not the identity of either or both of the companies remains or whether a new company is set up to own them. The Business Statistics Office (BSO) uses the term 'merger' only to refer to the last of these alternatives. A *reverse takeover* occurs when a smaller company takes over a larger one, as where a large unquoted company reverses into a smaller listed one. In fact both reverse takeovers and true mergers are rare events though the latter as a legal term has significance in European merger legislation. The vast majority of acquisitions, at least among quoted companies, are of a smaller company by a larger one where the terms 'takeover' or 'acquisition' are more accurate. The participants in an acquisition often use the term 'merger' to imply a coming together of equals, but even in the rare cases where the companies involved are of roughly equal size, one management group almost invariably dominates in the post-merger organisation. However, the term 'merger' does have a useful distinctive and technical accounting meaning where the shares of the acquirer are exchanged for those of the acquiree instead of the consideration being paid in cash (where the term 'acquisition' is used in this specific accounting sense: see Chapter 3 below).

A number of terms are used in this report to categorise acquisitions. *Horizontal acquisitions* occur where the parties are engaged in the same broad sector of industry or commerce, such as motor manufacture or food retailing - that is, when they are actual or potential market competitors.

(The qualification is necessary because they may not be in the same segment of the sector: as we shall show in Chapter 7, one of the problems which bedevils our present competition policy is the difficulty of defining a market.) *Vertical acquisitions* occur when the parties are actual or potential suppliers or customers, as when a motor manufacturer acquires a producer of electrical components or body parts. A *conglomerate* or *diversifying acquisition* occurs when a company in one sector, for example tobacco, acquires a company in another, for example frozen food.

Acquisitions may also be classified according to the nationality of the acquirer or the acquiree and the location of the target. In this report, *domestic acquisitions* are those of UK companies, either by other UK companies or by foreign companies, and *overseas acquisitions* are those of foreign companies based abroad by UK companies. These distinctions are important because the totals of UK acquisitions and merger activity issued by the BSO and commonly quoted include only UK acquisitions and mergers by UK companies: they do not include acquisitions of UK companies by foreign companies or overseas acquisitions (see Chapter 3).

We follow the BSO in making a distinction between mergers and acquisitions and *sales of subsidiaries between company groups*. The latter do not involve a change in the ownership of the *enterprise* (one or more subsidiaries or establishments under common ownership) but only the sale and acquisition of part of it: they are therefore conceptually distinct from takeovers, which result in the complete loss of control of the enterprise by its shareholders. There are two other categories of *divestment* which both result in the creation of a new and independent enterprise.[1] The first is the *spin-off* and the second the *sell-off*. A spin-off occurs where a quoted company floats off part of its activities as a separate quoted company. A sell-off occurs when an enterprise disposes of a subsidiary or activity, either to its existing management (a *management buy-out* [MBO], or to a group of outside managers (a *management buy-in* [MBI]).

Finally, takeovers can be categorised as *contested* and *agreed* or, synonymously, as *hostile* or *friendly*. A contested takeover is one in which a bid for control is made without the prior agreement of the management of the target company, while in a friendly bid that agreement is obtained before the event.

In this report we are concerned only with acquisitions by quoted companies, and our focus is primarily upon contested takeovers of these companies. There are, of course, large numbers of acquisitions of unquoted companies and unincorporated businesses which are unreported in the press and therefore not captured in the BSO statistics. Bannock (1990),

---

[1]*Joint ventures*, where two or more companies set up a new, jointly-owned enterprise, may be a form of divestment where existing assets or activities are placed in the venture. The growth of international joint ventures is a striking feature of the past two decades and one which raises many public policy issues analogous to those raised by acquisitions, for which joint ventures may often be a strategic substitute. Joint ventures, however, lie outside the scope of our Inquiry.

in one of the papers commissioned for this Inquiry, estimates that the total number of acquisitions in the UK in 1988 was some 30,000 compared with 1,224 recorded by the BSO, but the vast majority of these are very small and the transfers of assets involved in these minor transactions do not raise matters of concern for public policy. Unquoted (and of course unincorporated) businesses cannot normally be the subject of a hostile bid, since the ownership of most of these businesses is in the hands of the managers; and, unlike quoted companies, minority shareholders in these companies cannot be forced to sell, while controlling shareholders are free to stipulate that shares may not be disposed of to third parties without being offered to them first.

Our focus upon hostile takeovers we justify mainly on the grounds that these generally raise in their most acute form the wider issues of the interests of the other stakeholders in the business in addition to the shareholders - those of employees, management, local communities and the national economic interest - although the need to restrict the scope of our very broad field of inquiry is also a consideration. Contested bids have accounted for about one-third of all bids for quoted companies in the UK in the past five years. Despite this, agreed mergers also raise important issues of public interest and for this reason we do not neglect them entirely. Indeed one of the themes of our report, and one on which we elaborate in the next two chapters, is that the issues underlying all large takeovers are interrelated and deeply rooted in the separation of ownership and control of large enterprises which has steadily taken place in the last century.

II   The Aims of Takeovers

In an evolving economy, industrial organisation is never static: some enterprises are growing, some declining, new ones are set up and others go out of business. Existing businesses, moreover, have the choice between internalising functions or buying them in (vertical integration or disintegration) and between internal growth (expansion of existing activities or embarking on new ones) and external growth (acquisition). Among larger enterprises, failure followed by complete liquidation is a rare event; failure results in all or part of the business being acquired by others. Successful businesses may also wish to dispose of some of their activities (divestment) in order to concentrate their resources upon what is most profitable.

The choice between internal and external growth and vertical and horizontal integration or disintegration will be affected by many factors, including transaction costs, market growth, technology, competitive forces, and the cost and availability of managerial and financial resources. The last mentioned is of particular importance in determining the choice between internal and external growth. Large firms, and particularly quoted companies, are more likely to be able to pursue external growth because they have access to the necessary financial resources.

Economies of scale in finance are of considerable importance in determining industrial structure: large organisations can command finer terms in capital markets because perceived risks for investors are generally lower, while the fixed costs of new issues fall, as a proportion of total costs, the larger the issue. Small organisations have no access at all to securities markets and have to rely mainly upon their own resources, including those of families and friends and bank borrowing. It is because economies of scale in finance are so important that, as mentioned, large firms almost invariably acquire smaller ones. On the basis of a study of 1900 UK mergers, Franks and Harris (quoted in Fairburn and Kay 1989) reported that on average the acquirer is 7 to 8 times as large as the acquiree, based on market value of the equity.

Real, as distinct from financial, considerations are of course important, often crucially important, in determining corporate strategies on structure and growth. Changes in technology may alter the balance of advantage in favour of large versus small firms, and competitive forces may bring about changes in the degree and level of vertical and horizontal integration. We shall show later (in Chapter 2) that, paradoxically, in the UK the recent boom in mergers has been accompanied also by an increase in divestments and some reduction in vertical integration as larger firms have been buying in goods and services, from each other and from smaller firms, which hitherto were supplied in-house. These changes seem to have been brought about by the initially harsher and more competitive environment of the early 1980s as well as, in the case of divestments, potential or actual pressures from hostile takeover bids.

The forces determining economic structure and the role of mergers are complex and not fully understood, but it is not difficult to understand the attractions, from the point of view of the individual enterprise, of acquisition as a route for expansion.

The first point to make is that the acquisition of an existing business is a very rapid means of expansion, especially in a new field. Compared with the slow process of internal growth, which requires detailed planning, trial and error, recruitment of personnel, product development, investment in plant perhaps with long lead times, the building up of relationships with suppliers, the establishment of marketing strategies and channels of distribution, an acquisition which can be pushed through in a matter of weeks or months is fast indeed.

Of course these advantages of speed can only be enjoyed if a suitable acquisition is available, and this may not be the case in highly concentrated mature industries or in fragmented industries at an early stage in their development. In these cases internal growth or diversification by acquisition may be the only alternatives.

The second point to make in favour of an acquisition as an alternative to internal growth is that it is not only a faster but in many cases a cheaper alternative. Especially at low points in the stock market cycle, or when a bid target is in difficulty, the shares of acquisition targets normally trade at a substantial discount (40 per cent or more) to the replacement cost of their underlying assets. Investment in internal growth may, moreover, temporarily result in a fall in profits, while growth by acquisition can leave profitability unimpaired or even increased).

Most takeover bids seem to be motivated by a desire for expansion, or a wish to achieve a larger market share or even a dominant position. The rationale may be that the bidder can make more profitable use of the assets than the victim, either because he has superior management or because the acquisition will enable economies of scale in production, research or marketing to be exploited in the context of a larger group (synergy). In some cases bids are undoubtedly motivated by less rational considerations and there is evidence that pre-bid analysis of the victim is sometimes quite cursory. Accusations of irrationality have been directed at victims, as well as at bidders, where defending management have refused bids long after it would have best served the interests of their shareholders if they had accepted it. Some companies which have escaped takeover have not done conspicuously well since, and their shareholders would have done better to take the cash.

The motive for a bid may also be defensive (and it may be invited on similar grounds by the victim), either through a desire to make the acquiree's organisation larger as a protection against takeover, or to eliminate a competitor (perhaps one with desirable brands or products), or to allow some orderly reduction in industrial capacity, or all three of these motives.

Horizontal mergers pose the most obvious threat to competition, since by definition they reduce the number of established firms in an industry (though new sources of competition may arise from new entrants, including firms based abroad). Vertical mergers can also threaten competition, however, for example by placing a source of supply under the control of a competitor of firms that buy from it.

Some takeover bids are, of course, opportunistic and are made not as a part of a strategy for growth in a particular sector, but simply to exploit undervalued assets or to benefit from the high value placed upon the shares of the bidder. Some diversified holding companies (conglomerates) acquire and retain companies in a variety of industries; others attempt to buy and sell again at a profit, and some do both by retaining parts of their acquisitions and disposing of the remainder. Conglomerates are a classic illustration of the point made earlier about the importance of financial economies, since by definition they have no particular industrial expertise. It is interesting that conglomerates seem to thrive on capital market imperfections, where assets may not only be undervalued in these markets but where management in the acquirees find that capital is effectively available on better terms within a conglomerate group than it would be in the capital market as an independent concern.

Diversified acquisitions are made not only by conglomerates, of course. Companies of all kinds often acquire others in different fields so as to increase returns or to attempt to reduce risk. Most major international companies are now highly diversified. Various studies have shown that diversification increases with size of firm, as does merger activity. Even among the 200 largest UK manufacturing firms, Utton (1982) found that in 1988 on average 33 per cent of their output was accounted for by activities other than their principal one. This calculation was made on an individual plant basis. Companies may also diversify by takeover to improve their financial structure, for example to reduce gearing, or for tax reasons (see Chapter 3).

III   Takeover Strategy: the Bidder

In making an acquisition the target has to be identified and an assessment made of the maximum price that should be paid. Most large companies and all active conglomerates are continuously assessing the financial performance of their competitors or screening possible bid targets. Some bid targets are identified many years before a bid is actually made. The timing of the bid may be prompted by a favourable movement in the relative price-earnings (P/E) ratios of the bidder and the target. A company may prefer to bid for another when its own shares are highly valued in the market, or when the target's shares fall on bad annual results. Or the bidder may be forced to move by a bid from another quarter. If that bid is from a competitor, then the bidder may have an enhanced incentive to act so as to prevent the target falling into another competitor's hands. This was the case in the Nestlé takeover of Rowntree. Nestlé had reportedly identified Rowntree as a strategic target in 1986 but did not launch a bid until 1988, after its competitor Suchard had done so (Davis and Bannock 1990). Tax considerations may be a motivating factor in a bid (see Chapter 3).

In theory an acquisition is worth making if the present value of the future returns exceed the costs.[1] In practice, future returns and costs may be difficult to estimate. The bidder can make calculations based on the historical trend of returns for the target, adjusted for whatever synergistic benefits are expected - for example, closure of headquarter offices and surplus capacity, improved joint distribution, and so on. Obviously much can go wrong with these estimates: the costs of integrating the two companies may be higher than expected and the synergy less than expected. Financing costs or demand conditions may change: in the past two years some highly leveraged bids have run into trouble as interest rates have risen. In some cases the acquisition may not be what it appeared to be, as in for example Ferranti's disastrous acquisition of International Signal and Imperial's purchase of Howard Johnson, both in the United States. The most successful acquisitions from the bidder's point of view have

---

[1]The net present value of any business undertaking is the sum of future cash flows discounted at the firm's cost of capital minus the costs. Alternatively the internal rate of return (IRR) may be calculated, at which the net present value is zero, and this return compared with the firm's cost of capital. Subject to some technical qualifications, if the IRR is higher than the cost of capital, the project is worth undertaking.

generally been those where the bid target was in trouble but on the point of recovery, or where substantial assets could be unbundled and disposed of to meet all or part of the acquisition cost. Hanson Trust has shown exceptional skill in prejudging situations of these kinds.

Having carried out the valuation and decided on timing, the bidder has to decide upon the terms to be offered. If the price offered is a high one then the chances of an agreed bid are enhanced. An agreed bid is preferable to a contested bid for several reasons. Contested bids are costly not only because the defence usually results in a better price for the shares, but also because fees to advisers, advertising and other costs can be very high in a prolonged struggle for control. An agreed bid is a particularly desirable objective where, as in the case of Rowntree, the target is well managed and the bidder wishes to retain the goodwill of the management.

The bid and defence costs incurred in takeover activity are astonishingly high. Morgan (1990A) notes that Hoylake was reported to have spent £140 million on its abortive bid for BAT. Costs include fees and commissions to merchant banks, fees to professional advisers, public relations consultants, advertising and mailing costs. Morgan quotes John Kay's conservative total estimate of £500 million for these costs of UK merger activity in 1986. This amounted to some 7 per cent of the BSO's estimate of the value of acquisitions in that year, but it would represent a much higher proportion of the value of contested bids, which account for between about 20 and 40 per cent of the number of bids for quoted companies. It should also be noted that these costs do not include the value of management time which, especially given its alternative uses, is considerable.

Whilst a high offer may in some, though by no means all, cases help to avoid a prolonged contest it could, of course, result in the bidder paying more than necessary. A low offer, on the other hand, may not only be rejected outright but it could encourage a counter-offer from another bidder.

Clearly, pitching the initial bid at the right level is a tricky job. What is certain is that in most cases the bid will have to be significantly more than the market price of the shares before the bid is made (or anticipated; in most cases something leaks out, and in the past, market prices have generally risen ahead of a bid). According to Franks and Harris (*op. cit.*), the average increase in the acquiree's share price in the six months beginning four months before the bid (both contested and uncontested bids) was 30 per cent, though it may be very much more in a contested bid: in the Rowntree-Nestlé case it was 130 per cent. Bid premia arise because the prices quoted in the market are for small quantities of shares; a bid for control will mean that a higher price is necessary to flush out sellers of major stakes in the target company, though it may also mean that the stock market has undervalued the shares and failed to include a sufficient allowance for the possibility of a bid.

Target companies share prices generally rise ahead of a bid not only because the bidder's intentions are anticipated but also because many bidders make a toe-hold investment in their target before the bid is announced. This may involve a further strategic decision; if the bidder acquires more than 3 per cent of the equity then the target company must be informed, and if 30 per cent or more is acquired then the City Code requires the bidder to make an offer for the remaining shares.[1] The acquisition of a significant stake ahead of the offer may enable the potential bidder to reduce the average cost of his share purchases in the victim if the bid is successful. A toe-hold stake will also provide a capital gain if he is outbid by a competitor, as was the case for Suchard in its failed bid for Rowntree. Against this there is the risk that if the target is successful in fighting off any bid then the bid premium will disappear, leaving the unsuccessful bidder locked in with a capital loss. The bidder also has to decide whether or not to buy up to a 30 per cent stake in a 'dawn raid', as in the case of the initial bid by Suchard for Rowntree before which Suchard acquired a 12 per cent stake in the first hour of a day's trading.

The bidder also has to decide not only the value of his offer, but the form it will take: cash, equity shares or loan stock in cash, equity shares, convertible stock, or a combination of these. There are many aspects to consider here, including taxation, accounting considerations, the relative P/E ratios and capital structures of the bidder and target companies, the preferences of the vendors of the target's shares, and the wishes of the bidder's own shareholders, who may not wish to see their ownership diluted.[2] Even where the vendors prefer cash, as institutions often do, so as to retain the freedom to balance their portfolios and because, unlike individual shareholders, they may not be concerned with the need to avoid capital gains taxation,[3] it may be possible for the bidder to issue shares which can be converted into cash by an intermediary via what is known as a vendor placing.

In fact in recent years the proportion of total expenditure on UK acquisitions accounted for by cash has fluctuated sharply, from 26 per cent in 1986 to 82 per cent in 1989. Although several attempts have been made, academic studies, as in other aspects of the takeover process, have not been able to explain changes in the means of payment in takeovers satisfactorily either in the UK or the US (see Franks, Harris and Mayer in Auerbach 1988).

If the bidder is unable to persuade the management of the target company to recommend the bid, then he faces the task of convincing the shareholders that it is in their interest to accept a hostile bid. The dialogue

---

[1]Since the early 1980's following the first cases of the dawn raid technique, the limit for an initial, instantaneous purchase has been 15 per cent. An acquirer may not buy further shares within the following seven years.

[2]The provisions of the City Code may also affect the form of the consideration. A company owning 30 per cent and making an offer for the remainder must include a cash alternative, as must one having acquired 15 per cent or more during the 12 months prior to an offer.

[3]Where the target's shares are exchanged for shares in the bidder, no capital gains arises until the shares are sold. However, institutional shareholders - pension funds, for example - may not be liable for capital gains tax as trustees for their members.

takes the form of a paper war in which both parties will communicate with shareholders by post and, in the case of institutional shareholders, by person to person lobbying. These means will, as the struggle proceeds, usually be supplemented by press advertising and attempts to influence media comment. The bidder may also have to attempt to persuade the Office of Fair Trading that the bid should not be referred to the MMC and also to influence other stakeholders, such as the employees' Trade Unions, in its favour.

In its offer document and subsequently, the bidder may choose to emphasise either the shortcomings in the record of the existing management or, as in the Nestlé-Rowntree case, argue that the synergy between the companies is such that it could do better if the two were combined; or it may emphasise both. The bidder may argue, as in the case of the Hoylake bid for BAT, that the shareholders would benefit if the target company were re-structured and some of its assets disposed of or refloated. The thrust of the argument will have to be related to the means of payment offered: if it is purely a cash offer, then shareholders have to be convinced that it is a generous one; if it involves stock in the bidder, then shareholders also have to be convinced that the prospects of the bidder are more attractive than those of the target.

Offer documents have frequently been criticised for their lack of detail about the future plans of the bidder for the target and exactly how it would improve performance (see Morgan & Morgan 1990 for the views of the institutions in the survey commissioned for this Inquiry). In some cases, no doubt, this vagueness may be attributable to an insufficiency of information or lack of thought by the bidder, whose motives may not require radical change in the efficiency or strategy of management of the target, but it may reflect a desire to avoid attracting a competitive bid by revealing what a bargain the target really is. Another justification for vagueness about future plans may be a desire to avoid the unnecessary alienation of employees and other stakeholders. (It may, of course, as in the Nestlé/Rowntree case, be necessary to give assurances on employment and other matters in order to secure the ultimate approval of the incumbent management for a revised bid).

IV Takeover Strategy: the defence and the balance of power

Having decided to reject friendly overtures (if any), the victim of a hostile bid has a number of weapons at his disposal. The main thrust will be to argue that the bid undervalues the company. In its defence, Rowntree placed heavy emphasis on the unique value of its brands, the absence of alternative bid targets in its field, and its outstanding record for innovation in confectionery.

Assets may be revalued and a profit forecast prepared under the procedures set out in the City Code. The management will also justify its past record and may be able to reveal hitherto undisclosed developments and fresh intentions. The statements issued by Currys in its attempt to stave off a bid by Dixons in 1984, for example, revealed that there would be a 40 per cent increase in selling space in the following two years and that among other initiatives the group would sell and lease back some of its property, returning cash to shareholders (Cooke 1986, on whom we have drawn extensively in this section).

The target company will also reject the arguments in the bidder's offer document and, where appropriate, may criticise the bidder's own record. Rowntree were able to demonstrate that Nestlé's branded food products were threatened by private label products offered by the large multiples and that, while strong in the slow-growing block chocolate segment, Nestlé had failed to innovate in the rapidly expanding countline segment of confectionery where Rowntree's success lay. The target company will also try to demonstrate that the shareholders' interests will be better served if the company remains independent.

Reference to the MMC is an external factor which may intervene to avert a takeover. However, relatively few mergers are referred. Between 1985–89, of those that were referred, only 12 per cent were blocked completely and 26 per cent were abandoned and not reported on (Morgan and Morgan 1990). A reference therefore reduces the chance of a successful bid by about one third.

Most mergers simply do not qualify for referral under the existing criteria, principally that which disallows mergers which would create or enhance a monopoly (defined as a market share of 25 per cent: see Chapter 6). In the Rowntree case, the OFT did not recommend referral apparently on the grounds that Nestlé's UK market share in chocolate confectionery was very small (although the combined share of the two companies was well over 30 per cent) and rejected the defender's argument that Nestlé's relatively small share was the justification for the bid and that if Nestlé were successful, a strong potential competitor would be eliminated. The OFT also rejected as irrelevant Rowntree's non-reciprocity argument that Nestlé was itself bid-proof. Rowntree finally made representations to the European Commission which also decided not to intervene.

Another defence against a hostile bid is for the target management to give its support to a bid from a 'white knight' - another company with which management has more sympathy, perhaps because the new bidder's plans for the target are closer to their own. In 1983, for example, BAT intervened to outbid the German insurance group Allianz in the struggle for control of Eagle Star. Yet another tactic is for the target to steal the bidder's clothes by undertaking to carry out some or all of his plans. Ironically, in 1990 BAT were able to fight off the bid from Hoylake which wanted to increase shareholder value through a break-up of BAT's conglomerate interests by promising some disposals. In the Nestlé/Rowntree case the recommended bid-premium on offer was probably too high for any successful counter-bid, although discussions were held with Cadbury-Schweppes and others.

Some defensive tactics used in the USA are effectively ruled out in the UK by the City Code. These include the placing of shares in friendly hands, the sale of a highly valued asset ('crown jewel') or the issue of convertible securities which would ultimately dilute the bidder's shares ('poison pills'), expensive changes to termination compensation packages for executives ('golden parachutes').

The defending directors have some important advantages: they are better informed than the bidder about their own company and they can call upon the loyalty of their shareholders. As Lawrie (1990) points out, the inertia of the average shareholder favours the defence; though institutional shareholders, who now predominate, tend to be less inert than the private individual. The percentage of 'dead' shareholder accounts, which rest with the defence and cannot be used by the bidder to claim control, may be crucial.

Nevertheless, the balance of advantage probably lies with the bidder. The bidder, again following Lawrie, can time his bid to exploit a temporary weakness in the target's performance and share price which, perhaps following heavy investment, is on the verge of recovery, while the bidder's shares may be exceptionally strong. The bidder's advantage of surprise may allow him to prepare for a complex struggle in advance. Typically, the target in a hostile bid will be plunged into hectic activity with little warning, and our review of the takeover process in this chapter shows that there is a great deal to be done.

In the Rowntree case, Suchard, as mentioned, acquired 12 per cent of the company's equity in a dawn raid on April 13th 1988, giving institutional shareholders little time to assess the situation. By early May Suchard had still not made a bid but had acquired almost 30 per cent, and Nestlé had made a bid on April 26th. The chief executive of Rowntree had been in South Africa on April 13th when his company's future was put into play. He was to have only ten weeks until June 23rd, when Rowntree management finally agreed to recommend the revised bid from Nestlé, although the real battle to remain independent was lost within a month of the Suchard bid.

A further disadvantage for the defending directors is that while they have to persuade their own shareholders that they should hold onto their shares rather than sell them at the premium generally required to win control, the bidder may not need to consult its own shareholders, at least until after the event. Nestlé shareholders were not in fact consulted at all in the acquisition of Rowntree.

2 The Scale of Merger Activity

I Sources of statistics

There are two main sources of statistics on merger activity: those based on press reports and counts derived from regulatory procedures. Neither type is comprehensive, since not all small mergers are reported in the press and regulation is only concerned with large mergers. Like all statistics, data on mergers need to be interpreted with care and there are many pitfalls for the unwary. For example, the data may cover announced bids or realised acquisitions, and may or may not include financial companies and foreign takeovers. The coverage and definition of merger statistics are described, together with a detailed analysis of the available data, in Bannock (1990A), a study carried out for this Inquiry and upon which we draw in this chapter.

The most frequently used series on mergers for the UK are those published by the BSO which are based on press counts. In the remainder of this report, unless stated otherwise, we use the BSO series of the value of acquisitions of independent companies and sales of subsidiaries between company groups. This series covers only industrial and commercial companies (financial companies are excluded) and only acquisitions of UK companies by UK companies (acquisitions of UK companies by overseas companies are not included). The BSO series also does not include management buy-outs (MBOs) (where the management acquires a subsidiary from its parent) or management buy-ins (MBIs) (where a subsidiary is acquired not by another company group but by a group of independent managers). Table 2.1 puts these various inclusions and exclusions into the context of the total number and value of all transfers of businesses in the UK (though this total will still exclude many small transfers and all UK acquisitions abroad). Acquisitions of independent enterprises are the largest element in the total, accounting for 57 per cent by value, most of this (perhaps 80 per cent or more) being the value of quoted companies acquired. Together with sales of subsidiaries between company groups (which do not involve the extinction of an independent enterprise), the BSO series covers 75 per cent of the value of transfers of businesses. Acquisitions of UK companies by foreign companies, which include both enterprises and subsidiaries, are only about 11 per cent of the value of domestic acquisitions and inter-company sales, and 8 per cent of all transfers of businesses. (The 1988 figure was in fact exceptionally high because it included the acquisition of Rowntree).

The combined value of MBOs and MBIs which result in the creation of an independent enterprise from a subsidiary was very considerable (17 per cent of transfers) and in fact represented a peak, although there was a fall in 1989. Finally, UK acquisitions abroad greatly exceeded the number and value of foreign acquisitions in the UK. Comparisons of cross-border acquisitions over time are difficult because of changes in the coverage of the data, but there is no evidence that inward acquisitions are increasing faster than outward acquisitions, or as a proportion of domestic merger activity.

Table 2.1   TRANSFERS OF 'SIGNIFICANT' UK BUSINESSES, 1988

	Number	%	Value £m	%
1. Sales of subsidiaries between UK company groups	287	16.1	5253.2	17.8
2. Acquisitions by UK companies	937	52.6	16869.4	57.1
'BSO Series'	1224	68.7	22122.6	74.9
3. Acquisitions of UK-by-overseas companies	76	4.3	2484.0	8.4
4. MBOs	372	20.9	3717.0	12.6
5. MBIs	110	6.2	1230.0	4.2
Total UK transfers of business	1782	100.0	29553.6	100.0
6. Memo: Acquisitions of overseas companies by UK companies	444		5547.0	

SOURCE   1, 2, 3 & 6: Business Monitor, MQ7;
4 & 5: Nottingham Centre for Management Buy-Out Research

II   Trends in the UK

Merger activity in the UK in 1989 was at an all-time peak since the BSO series began in 1954. This remains true even if expenditure on acquisitions is expressed in real terms. Comparisons of the number and value of mergers over time, however, even at constant prices do not allow for the growth of the economy. We prefer for this reason to look at expenditure on acquisitions expressed as a percentage of the Gross Domestic Product (GDP).

Figure 2.2 also shows that in the recent merger boom the average real size of acquisitions has increased compared with earlier peaks. This does not seem to reflect the impact of just a few very large mergers in each year, but an increase in the number of acquisitions over £25 million which is a great deal more than would be expected from the effects of inflation.

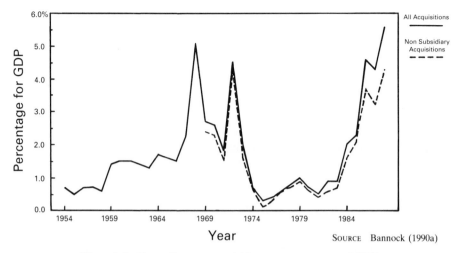

Figure 2.1   Expenditure on acquisitions as a percentage of GDP

Bannock (1990) updates some earlier calculations by Hannah (1975) who constructed a series of expenditure on acquisitions in manufacturing going back to 1890. This series does show that as a percentage of GDP, post-war merger waves in the UK have been vastly greater than those of the earlier period.

Figure 2.2 also shows that in the recent merger boom the average real size of acquisitions has increased compared with earlier peaks. This does not seem to reflect the impact of just a few very large mergers in each year, but an increase in the number of acquisitions over £25 million which is a great deal more than would be expected from the effects of inflation.

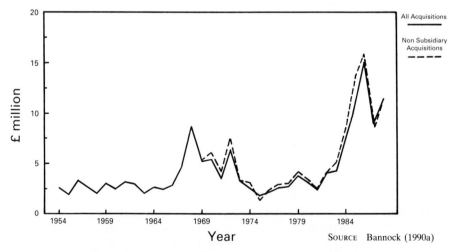

Figure 2.2   Real expenditure per acquisition, UK 1954–88

Finally, it is well known that the ebbs and flows in merger activity that can be seen in our charts are positively related to stock market price indices; that is to say expenditure on acquisitions tends to rise when share prices increase, and to fall when share prices fall (Figure 2.3). This seems to be true not only for the UK but also for the United States and other countries. The explanation of this relationship seems to be simply that business people pursue expansion by acquisition most actively when profit prospects and market sentiment are favourable. More complex hypotheses, such as those based upon varying relationships between the prices of first (larger) and second line (smaller company) stocks, have not proved verifiable in practice.

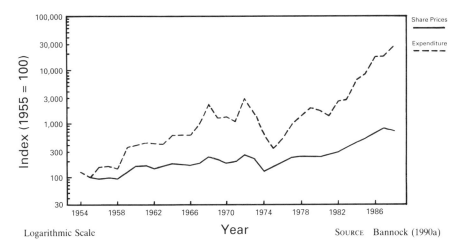

Figure 2.3   Expenditure on acquisitions and share prices, UK 1954–88

III   Comparisons with other countries

International comparisons of merger activity are quite difficult to make because of differences in the coverage of the available statistics. However, it is very clear that merger activity occurs on a much larger scale in the UK and the United States (and probably also in Australia and Canada) than in France and Japan, and probably also than in Germany. Bannock (1990), for example, calculates that expenditure on acquisitions in 1988, including inward acquisitions, was 5.3 per cent of GDP in the UK, 5.1 per cent in the United States, 1.9 per cent in France and 0.9 per cent in Japan.

Merger activity has increased everywhere in the current wave. Only for the United States are long-term comparisons possible with the UK. These comparisons show that, unlike the UK, the recent peak in the US is not an all-time high. Although the number of acquisitions in the US is higher in the current boom than in earlier waves, the value of assets acquired as a percentage of GDP has never returned to the record levels of the 1890s.

IV The role of banks and other financial institutions

The principal reason for the difference in the level of takeover activity between the so-called Anglo-Saxon and other countries seems to lie in the different roles of the banks in these two groups of countries. In the UK and the US the commercial banks, except in their roles as trustees (see Chapter 3), are not significant holders of equity, while in Germany and Japan they are; and in France and Italy the state is also an important shareholder in industrial, commercial and financial companies.[1] In both groups of countries, larger companies are no longer owner-managed to any significant extent (Chapter 3), but in the Anglo-Saxon countries ownership is largely concentrated in the hands of financial institutions such as pension funds, mutual trusts and insurance companies, while in the other countries it is to a much greater extent in the hands of banks or in state holdings.

These different types of financial institutions adopt, and indeed are obliged to adopt, a different attitude towards the companies in which they have investments. Pension funds, insurance companies and mutual funds hold shares as investments on behalf of those who place their savings with them. Their duty is to balance risk against the maximisation of returns on the savings in their care. These institutions are, in short, passive investors, in the sense that they do not normally become involved in the management of individual companies, though they do switch holdings or add to or reduce holdings in the interest of portfolio management.[2]

Banks, by contrast, except where they are acting as trustees, have a different interest in the businesses in which they invest. Their investments are made in the interests of their own shareholders and they will be acting as bankers to the companies in which they hold shares. These banks have a vital and long-term interest in their investments, since what is at stake is not only the performance of the shares but also the banking relationship itself. A takeover bid could lead to loss of business for the bank, and the failure of a company in which the bank holds shares could result not only in the loss of that investment but the writing-off of loans to that company.

These differences of interest go a long way to explain the lower level of takeover activity in countries in which banks rather than other financial institutions are predominant owners of equity. Where a large bank customer gets into trouble or performs poorly, the bank has a strong

---

[1] In the United States, commercial banks are prohibited from acting as investment banks by the Glass-Steagal Act (1933), though in the UK and Germany there are no legal impediments of this kind. In Japan, banks are limited to 5 per cent holdings in industrial and commercial companies.

[2] Individual private shareholders are, of course, except where they are directly involved in the management of the company, also likely to be passive in this same sense as institutions.

incentive to use its influence to change the management and, if necessary, to make more loans or convert loans to equity. Indeed, historically much of the ownership of industry by banks (and the state, which has analogous motivations) in European countries arose during the economic difficulties during the inter-war period when banks were forced to acquire failing business customers.

There are, of course, other differences which have affected the level of takeover activity. Regulations on the disclosure of share ownership and accounting information have been generally less stringent or not enforced in many continental European countries, making the task of the predator in identifying and assessing bid targets more difficult. The widespread use of bearer shares and of non-voting shares also has in the past made it difficult or impossible for a bidder to gain control.[1] In some countries restrictive provisions in company articles act as a bar to takeovers by foreign-based companies, as for example was the case for Nestlé. Generally speaking, the importance of the unquoted company and unincorporated business sector, which is not amenable to hostile bids, is greater outside the Anglo-Saxon countries, while the stock market plays a larger role in business finance in the UK and the US. Despite some expansion in the 1980s, the small business sector in the UK in particular remains smaller than in most, if not all, other advanced countries. Enterprises with a turnover of less than £30 million, for example, according to a recent estimate, account for only about 32 per cent of private sector GDP (excluding the primary sector) in the UK, compared with 46 per cent in FR Germany (Bannock 1991B). The role of small business is greater still in Japan. Whatever the source of the relatively poor postwar performance of industry in Britain, it cannot be the result of too few large firms. Of the 400 world's largest industrial enterprises in 1973, 211 were US-based, 50 British, 29 German, 28 Japanese and 24 French (Chandler 1990).

V   Mergers and Concentration

It is to be expected that if companies operating in the same product markets merge (horizontal mergers), then market concentration (the market shares of the largest competitors) will increase unless the sales of existing smaller companies and new entrants increase faster than theirs do. Over the long term, average market concentration in Britain has increased, at least up to the late 1970s, and mergers have certainly contributed to this process - though for technical reasons it is difficult to say by precisely how much. Hart and Clarke (1980) on the basis of

---

[1]Uniformity in regulations on the disclosure of share ownership is the objective of the *Directive on Substantial Holdings* (88/627/CEE). Once the member states have implemented this directive, and in so far as it is enforced, their holders of 10 per cent or more will have to disclose their interests to the company.

case studies concluded that mergers were responsible for some 50 per cent of the average increase in market concentration between 1958 and 1968.

The calculation of the precise effect of mergers upon aggregate concentration (the share of a given number of the largest enterprises in total sales or output) is also difficult. Aggregate concentration has also been increasing, however. Prais (1976) showed that the share of the 100 largest enterprises in UK manufacturing net output rose from 16 per cent in 1909 to about 41 per cent in 1970. The comparable figures for the United States were 22 per cent in 1909 and 33 per cent in 1970. For Germany, Prais estimated that aggregate concentration was about one-third lower than in Britain in the late 1960s. Between 1970 and 1988 there appears to have been a slight fall in aggregate concentration in UK manufacturing, of something in excess of two percentage points (Bannock and Peacock 1987), but it seems quite probable that the recent merger boom will have reversed this decline and indeed there were signs of this in 1987 (the latest figures available) (Table 2.2). Little is known about changes in aggregate concentration outside manufacturing. It has certainly increased in retailing and probably in other sectors such as hotels and catering, vehicle distribution and servicing, estate agencies and financial services, for example. Certainly, as we shall show, aggregate concentration measured by market capitalisation has increased in the quoted company sector as a whole.

Table 2.2 SHARE OF THE 100 LARGEST PRIVATE SECTOR ENTERPRISES IN MANUFACTURING NET OUTPUT, UK 1909–87

Year	%
1988	37.7
1987	36.5
1986	39.1
1985	38.3
1984	38.7
1983	41.4
1982	41.0
1981	40.6
1980	40.5
1970	40.5
1968	41.0
1963	37.0
1958	32.0
1953	27.0
1949	22.0
1935	24.0
1924	22.0
1909	16.0

SOURCES   1909–70, Prais (1976)
1980–85, *Report on the Census of Production*, BSO, updated from Bannock and Peacock (1989). There are some differences in coverage between Prais' data and those for later years which are for SIC(80)2–4.

Various estimates have been made of the contribution of acquisitions to the growth of aggregate concentration. Aaronovitch and Sawyer put it at 54 per cent for the period 1958–67 among a population of quoted companies in manufacturing and distribution (Alan Hughes in Fairburn & Kay 1989).

In Britain between 1973 and 1988 the number of domestic quoted UK companies fell by 43 per cent to 2054. Over 58 per cent of the listing cancellations followed acquisitions (the rest were at request or for other reasons, for example liquidation). The number of new listings of domestic companies has been insufficient to replace those disappearing through acquisition, even if new flotations on the unlisted markets (the USM and the now defunct Third Market) are included (Bannock 1990A). Increased aggregate concentration is, of course, overwhelmingly the result of the increasing size of quoted companies. Within the quoted sector, the share of the 100 largest companies in total listed market capitalisation has increased from 65.2 per cent in 1984 to 67.3 per cent in 1990, after falling to 60.5 per cent in 1988. (FTSE 100 market capitalisation as a percentage of total market capitalisation (list plus USM). Source: The International Stock Exchange, London.) The quoted company sector is therefore also becoming more concentrated.

VI The future scale of merger activity

The slowdown in economic activity and the end of the stock market boom in the late 1980s seem to have brought an end to the boom in mergers as we enter 1991. We have seen that successive merger waves have in the past led to an increase in market and aggregate concentration in the UK. We do not yet know for sure whether the recent boom will have had the same effect, but it seems probable that it will have done so. Is there a prospect then of a further merger wave with further increases in concentration later on in the 1990s when economic prospects and stock market prices again improve?

A ratchet-like increase in mergers and concentration is not inevitable. In the United States there was no increase in aggregate concentration in US manufacturing between 1963 and 1977 (Auerbach 1988), despite a merger boom in the 1960s. In the UK there was a slight fall in concentration in the middle 1980s, though this seems to have been arrested and possibly reversed subsequently, as the recent merger boom heightened. What was common to both these experiences was a high rate of economic growth and new business formation.

In addition to new business formation and the growth of businesses below the concentration measure threshold, however, divestments of earlier acquisitions also help to offset the effects of mergers upon concentration. As we showed at the beginning of this chapter, divestments including sales of subsidiaries (spin-offs) amounted to only 35 per cent of the total value of transfers of business in 1988. Spin-offs do not necessarily reduce concentration and, although no data are available, it is probable that a large proportion represent sales of subsidiaries by very large companies to other large companies. Indeed, where the motive of these sales has been a desire to reduce unrelated diversification, in many cases such sales may increase market concentration. This is because some companies reduce diversification while others improve their market share by acquiring new subsidiaries which are in their own line of business.

The value of MBOs and MBIs has recently been similar in magnitude to that of spin-offs, however, and this type of divestment does reduce concentration because it results in the creation of a new independent enterprise. Although spin-offs have shown some tendency to increase as a percentage of acquisitions, MBOs and MBIs increased spectacularly in the 1980s and were, in fact, virtually unknown in the UK until the late 1970s (Bannock 1990C).

The growth of divestments, and particularly of MBOs and MBIs, is a new feature in the economies of the advanced countries. Chandler (1990) refers to divestments (variously described as 'downsizing' and 'deglomeration') and to the market for corporate control as new major features of the world economy. Widespread large-scale divestments first began in the United States in the early 1970s and followed in the UK rather later. They seem too now to be spreading, along with an increase in merger activity, to the non-Anglo Saxon countries.

There seem to be several forces behind the increase in divestment, but they can all be summed up in the intensification of competition which in Britain followed the recession in the early 1980s; and more generally through the impact of Japanese, and to some extent European-based firms, on global markets. Chandler ascribes the enhanced motive for divestment to the overload on the decision-makers in top management of large and diversified companies. Part of it, however, also resulted from the need to reduce the scope of in-house activities where products and services could be more economically bought-in than provided in-house. The spinning-off of these activities, not merely those carried out in separate subsidiaries, provided new opportunities for smaller firms. This helps to explain the enormous increase in new business formation which took place in the UK (and the US) in the 1980s.[1] Another factor was the desire to reduce the vulnerability of companies to unwelcome takeover bids.

In addition to a sea change in corporate attitudes towards diversification and a new determination to return to core activities, the 1980s also saw the beginnings of a revaluation of business enterprise as such. Smaller firms benefited from more favourable government policies, and new business formation increased in a spectacular way. At first the rate of business start-ups seemed to have been stimulated by the 1981 recession

---

[1]The lower levels of vertical integration which have resulted from more buying-in of goods and services from smaller firms are bringing the structure of UK business more in line with that of other countries.

and unemployment, but in fact it had begun earlier and continued to accelerate to the end of the decade.[1] The vast majority of these start-ups were very small and many will founder in the current recession, but a few should survive to become more substantial enterprises in the 1990s.

We cannot predict to what level the next takeover boom will rise, but it seems unlikely, whatever changes have taken place in attitudes to diversification, that the latent appetite for horizontal mergers will have been much affected by recent developments. Nor does it seem likely that, on present policies in the UK or Europe, regulation will prove to be a very strong countervailing force. (While never very determined in Europe, merger policy in the US, which appeared successfully to restrain concentration in the 1960s and 1970s, seems to have softened considerably in the past decade - see George Hay in Fairburn and Kay 1989.)

VII   Do Mergers Matter?

Before moving on in the next chapter to look further into the underlying balance of forces for and against the growth of merger activity, this is an appropriate point to pause and ask: do mergers matter? We return to this question more fully and ask what, if anything, should be done about it, in our conclusions in Chapter 8.

In themselves, mergers do not immediately create new national wealth; they simply result in a transfer of the ownership, and normally also the management, of existing assets. Unless these assets are employed more efficiently by their new owners than they were before, then nothing will have been gained while real resources will have been wasted in the process of transfer, especially in contested bids. Highly geared takeover bids may, if post-merger performance is not improved sufficiently to service the debt, threaten the survival of previously viable businesses. From the point of view of economic welfare, internal growth is generally preferable to growth by acquisition because the former will mean pressing against the efforts of competitors, who may be stimulated to perform better; or by innovation, or both.

The intensity of competition may not be diminished by horizontal mergers; it may be enhanced if the new group offers a greater threat to other firms in the industry. Frequently, however, a horizontal acquisition will reduce competitive pressure on the acquirer, and it will always reduce the number of decision centres and hence the potential sources of innovation and change. This is also why aggregate concentration matters, and it matters particularly where larger firms are able to take over smaller ones - not because they are more efficient in their use of real resources, but because they are able to command greater financial resources at a lower

---

[1]These changes in corporate policies, enterprise culture and new business formation are described in Bannock and Peacock (1989) and Bannock (1991A).

cost. Economies of scale in finance do not translate into real savings in resources independently of the uses to which the finance is put. The lower borrowing costs of large firms reflect lower interest rates, but interest rates are a transfer price, not a resource cost. These financial economies simply translate into shifts of income between groups of savers and borrowers, leaving national net output unaffected (Scitovsky 1951).[1]

It is often argued that even market concentration does not matter in a country like the UK which is exposed to actual and potential competition from producers in other countries. But the quality and degree of domestic competition remains vitally important for the success of domestic industry which, for example, remains dependent upon the competitiveness of its domestic suppliers, even though that industry may be competing abroad and suffering from imports. Porter (1990) shows that Japanese success in export markets in virtually every case has been built upon fierce domestic competition.[2] Porter also argues that small static gains in efficiency (if any) arising from mergers are easily lost in the blunting of rivalry that results in diminished pressures for dynamic improvement. Finally, in recent years less than half of UK acquisitions involving companies with assets below £30 million have been in the non-manufacturing sector in which there is little or no competition from abroad.

Neither the study of the progress of individual companies which have been involved in merger activity, nor comparisons between the performances of merger-intensive Anglo-Saxon countries and those where mergers are less common, give support to the belief that mergers are generally beneficial. In view of the effect of mergers on concentration it is therefore surprising that the third and largest post-war merger boom in the UK has aroused so little criticism and concern.

---

[1] This analysis is only strictly correct in a closed economy. The ability of large companies to borrow more cheaply overseas can, on certain assumptions, result in real resource savings.

[2] The importance of a significant number of domestic competitors as a cause of competitive strength was easily forgotten in merger waves in the face of heady arguments that 'we need bigger units to compete with the Americans' (1960s) '...the Japanese' (1970s and 80s) and more recently, 'in Europe after 1992'. Today the UK has only one major indigenous car producer, now part of British Aerospace: in 1950 it had six, fewer than Japan has even today (9). Germany today has three (4 if Porsche is included), the vast US market three, and Italy one. Although mergers are frequently justified on the grounds of export competitiveness, it is difficult to think of any major international company anywhere which has gained sustained competitive advantage through acquisitions. A few have succeeded despite unsuccessful acquisitions (Volkswagen); many, by contrast, have prospered without significant acquisitions.

3 The Forces Favouring Takeovers

I The dynamics of scale

We saw in the previous chapter that although successive merger waves have not necessarily increased in scale in relation to the expanding economy, they have contributed to the emergence of giant firms and to high and increasing levels of aggregate concentration.

It is still generally supposed that very large firms are necessary to achieve optimal production economies of scale. This may have been true before World War II and even for some time afterwards, but it is certainly not, in general, true today. Prais (1976) found that the average number of plants owned by the 100 largest UK manufacturing enterprises rose from 27 to 72 between 1958 and 1972, while average employment per plant fell from 750 to 430. These trends have continued, and indeed may have accelerated since then.

Prais did find that multi-plant operation tended to result in increased market concentration and power, but the main benefits to companies were to be found elsewhere. Lower transport and communications costs have 'in this generation facilitated and extended the control by a head office of distant plants as much as the railway and the general post did in the last century' (Prais 1976). Lower advertising costs in large operations was also a factor, but the main advantages of the large firm over the small he found were financial, notably the ability to maintain higher levels of gearing and a lower cost of capital.

Prais did not examine claims that there are scale economies in research and development which justify giant firms (and mergers). This is not an issue which is as easily resolved because there are both conceptual and measurement problems in assessing the effects of scale upon invention and innovation, though it is clear that larger size is not a guarantee of innovative capability. It has been established that small firms contribute a disproportionately high share of innovations compared with their share of R&D expenditure (which may, however, be under-recorded) (Freeman 1982). Inventor-entrepreneurs with few resources have also contributed in the past to a large number of key inventions, from the jet engine to Xerography (Jewkes, Sawers and Stillerman 1969) and to this day in such varied fields as scientific instruments, food products, electronics and computer software. We know of no studies on the relationship between mergers and innovation, but common observation supports the view that large companies which have grown mainly by internal expansion (Rolls Royce Aero, Boeing, Sony, IBM, for example) have a more distinguished record in this respect than acquisitive companies.

II   The separation of ownership and control

It is not necessary for us to set out in detail the reasons for the economies of scale in finance which favour the acquisition of smaller companies by larger ones. This has been done elsewhere (for example in Prais 1976) and we pointed out the essential scale-related features of capital costs and availability in Chapter 1.[1]

Securities markets in the UK are now dominated by very large institutions which own the bulk of the capital that is listed in these markets, and by the large companies and institutions which have issued this capital. Although there are some 2,000 UK and Irish companies listed on the Stock Exchange with an equity market capitalisation of over £500 billion, the leading hundred of these included in the 100 FTSE Index account for 67 per cent and the largest 10 alone account for over 20 per cent.

It is important to note the surprising fact that in aggregate, the securities markets are not an important source of new equity capital funds for companies: in the past decade, in no single year have ordinary share issues accounted for as much as 10 per cent of the sources of capital funds, and the average has been less than half that amount. Moreover a large, though fluctuating, proportion of new share issues has been for the purposes of acquiring other listed companies, while some of the rest represents new capital for newly listed companies. The bulk of capital funds, about three quarters, typically comes from retained earnings and about one-fifth from debt, mostly bank borrowings. In this, UK companies are similar to those in other countries, though the role of bank borrowing is greater in the US and much greater in Germany (Table 3.1).

Just as most of the value of listed shares is attributable to those issued by very large companies, so most of them are now owned by large financial institutions. At the end of 1988, only about one quarter of the value of UK listed ordinary shares was owned by the personal sector (Morgan & Morgan 1990A). This proportion fell steeply, from 79 per cent in 1957 to 54 per cent in 1975 (excluding ownership by non-financial corporates). The gainers have been pension funds and insurance companies, which by 1988 accounted for 56 per cent (68 per cent if overseas and non-financial corporate holdings are excluded, as they are in Table 2).

---

[1]The fact that large companies take over small ones means that anything which encourages concentration will also stimulate mergers. Prais points out that even if the growth rates of firms in a given population were merely the result of random processes, then concentration would inevitably increase over time (Gibrat's Law).

Table 3.1 SOURCES OF FINANCE CIRCA 1980

	Debt	New Share Issues	Retained Earnings	Total
USA	%	%	%	%
Manufacturing	19.8	5.9	74.3	100.0
Other industry	48.5	3.8	47.7	100.0
Commerce	40.0	4.4	55.6	100.0
UK				
Total	19.3	4.4	76.3	100.0
FRG				
Manufacturing	43.5	4.9	51.6	100.0
Other industry	31.2	6.0	62.8	100.0
Commerce	49.6	4.4	46.1	100.0

SOURCE King & Fullerton 1984

The share of households in the ownership of corporate equity has also been falling in other countries, while ownership by financial institutions has been increasing. As shown in Table 3.2, in the US the proportion of corporate equity market value owned by households fell from 87 per cent in 1960 to 82 per cent in 1970 and to 74 per cent in 1980. The percentage holdings by tax-exempt institutions (primary pension funds and insurance companies) are twice as high in the UK as they are in the US or Germany.

Table 3.2 DOMESTIC OWNERSHIP OF CORPORATE EQUITY CIRCA 1980

	UK	US	FRG
	%	%	%
Households	43.5	74.3	73.1
Tax exempt institutions	40.7	21.5	20.7
Insurance companies	15.7	4.1	6.2
Total	100.0	100.0	100.0

NOTE Excludes non-financial corporate and overseas ownership.
SOURCE King & Fullerton 1984

What these figures mean is that the direct ownership of companies is shifting from individuals to financial institutions. This is not a new phenomenon; nor, as noted, is it restricted to the UK. In the 19th century, industry was owned predominantly by wealthy individuals and families who played a major role in the management of the businesses they owned. As stock markets developed to meet increasing capital needs, ownership became more dispersed - a process greatly accelerated after World War II - with rising tax rates on personal incomes and the growing importance of tax-sheltered institutional savings.

In a book published in 1932, Adolf Berle and Gardiner Means were the first to document the progressive concentration of economic power in the hands of a small number of companies and the dispersion of the ownership of these companies. They found that the share of corporate net income accounted for by the 200 largest US companies rose from 33 per cent in 1920 to 43 per cent in 1929. By the end of that period, in 44 per cent by number and 58 per cent by assets, no individual shareholder controlled more than 5 per cent of the equity, and these companies were effectively controlled not by the owners but by management. Berle and Means described this variously as the 'institution of passive property', 'the separation of ownership and control', and the emergence of 'collective capitalism'. (Later, Peter Drucker was to call it 'pension fund socialism').

In the revised edition of their book published in 1967 (Berle & Means 1967), the authors found that the process of concentration and separation of ownership and management had continued. The percentage of management-controlled companies, for example, had risen from 44 per cent in 1929 to 84.5 per cent in 1963. As we noted in Chapter 2, the concentration of output in the hands of the 100 largest companies has risen even higher in the UK than in the US. Prais (1976) found that in 1972, in 56 per cent of the top 100 UK manufacturing companies the members of the Board owned less than 0.5 per cent of the voting shares, and in 85 per cent the directors owned under 5 per cent.

Since the first edition of Berle & Means' book, however, there has been a further development and that is the re-concentration of ownership of large companies into the hands of a small number of financial institutions. As already shown, these institutions have steadily displaced individual private shareholders as the direct owners of shares. Although these institutions are managing the funds of large numbers of private individuals who largely remain the ultimate beneficiaries, their role is in effect to further increase the distance between the management of companies and their ultimate owners.

Scott (1986) has painstakingly identified the 20 largest shareholders in the 250 largest companies in Britain, the US and Japan (Table 3.3). In Britain these shareholders are principally pension funds and insurance companies; in the US they are to a greater extent the trust departments of banks, while in Japan (and also in Germany), banks are major beneficial shareholders in their own right. Except in Britain, all these shareholders are themselves among the top 250 industrial, commercial and financial companies, and in Japan there is extensive interlocking ownership.

In Britain and the US in particular, none of these individual institutional shareholdings amounts to control; they are all less than 10 per cent and generally less than half of that amount. Indeed, it is the policy of these shareholders to spread their funds over many holdings so as to spread risk: they are investors interested in the performance of their funds, and have neither the wish nor the means to become involved in the management of the companies in which these funds are invested.[1]

---

[1]According to a recent survey by the National Association of Pension Funds, nearly a quarter of pension funds have a policy of never using their shareholders' voting rights in companies in which they have a stake, while only 20 per cent have a policy of voting at all times. (Financial Times, 2nd March 1991.)

Table 3.3 THE 20 LARGEST SHARE PARTICIPANTS AND THE NUMBER OF THE TOP 250 COMPANIES IN WHICH THEY HAVE HOLDINGS

BRITAIN 1976		USA 1980		JAPAN 1980	
Prudential Assurance	88	J.P. Morgan	81	Nippon Life Ins (Sa)	149
National Coal Board	75	Manufacturers Hanover	55	Dai-Ichi Mutual Life Ins	98
Co-operative Group*	64	TIAA	54	Dai-Ichi Kangyo Bank (D)	72
Legal & General Assurance	64	Wells Fargo	50	Industrial Bank of Japan	62
Norwich Union Assurance*	64	Citicorp	49	Fuji Bank (F)	58
Pearl Assurance	64	Bankers Trust	48	Mitsui Trust and Banking (Mi)	57
Barclays Bank	60	General Electric	42	Sumitomo Bank (Su)	52
Hill Samuel	55	United States Steel	37	Sanwa Bank (Sa)	50
Robert Fleming	52	Prudential Insurance	36	Asahi Mutual Life Ins	50
Electricity Council	48	Chase Manhattan	32	Meiji Mutual Life Ins (M)	48
Mercury Securities	48	First National Boston	29	Tokio Marine & Fire Ins (M)	47
Royal Insurance	46	National Detroit	28	Sumitomo Mutual Life (Su)	47
Shell Tpt & Trading	45	Continental Corp	25	Mitsui Bank (Mi)	45
National Westminster	44	Chemical NY Bank	24	Mitsubishi Trust & Banking (M)	41
Commercial Union Assurance	42	Bank America	23	Daiwa Bank	41
Britannic Assurance*	39	Mellon National Bank	23	Long Term Credit Bank	38
Midland Bank	39	First Chicago	23	Mitsubishi Bank (M)	36
Church Commissioners*	38	Bank of N.Y.	22	Tokai Bank	33
General Accident	38	Equitable Life	20	Mitsui Mutual Life Ins (Mi)	29
Save & Prosper	37	Du Pont	19	Sumitomo Trust & Banking (Sa)	27
* Not members of Top 250				*Aligned holdings:*	
				D = DKB	
				F = Fuyo	
				M = Mitsubishi	
				Mi = Mitsui	
				Sa = Sanwa	
				Su = Sumitomo	

SOURCE Scott 1986

The separation of ownership from control in the complex ways we have described means that managers of major companies, who typically control only a tiny proportion of the equity, have become vulnerable to the attentions of other groups of managers in other larger companies who command the resources to acquire a controlling stake in their company. As takeover bids promise attractive short-term gains to passive shareholders because a premium over the pre-bid price is normally required to gain control, the separation of ownership from control results in an in-built bias towards takeovers. This bias may be increased by the possibility of a divergence of the long term interests of owners and managers, the former being impressed by profitability, the latter by the exercise of power and the higher salaries and benefits that go with increasing corporate size. This so-called agency problem, which has much exercised the minds of economists, is discussed further in Chapter 4.

As we shall describe later, there are powerful forces working against takeovers. These include possible conflicts of interest between owners and managers arising from management's need to maintain profitability in order to reduce their vulnerability to external interference. There are, however, several other forces working in favour of takeovers, to which we shall now turn.

III Taxation

As mentioned above, the tax system has favoured indirect investment by individuals in companies via financial institutions rather than by direct share ownership. Pension premia by both employers and employees are deductible for tax purposes up to certain limits, while generally speaking the funds in which these premia are invested are sheltered from all taxation. Until 1984 life insurance premia were also subject to relief for income tax purposes in the UK, and capital gains under life policies also still receive favourable tax treatment. There are other ways in which the tax system favours indirect investment, for example Personal Equity Plans. These give investment in equity shares freedom from tax on both income from dividends and capital gains and, as they have to be managed by financial institutions, this effectively limits them to shares in larger companies, in investment trusts and units in unit trusts. Savers who choose to invest in shares directly, including shares in smaller unquoted companies, are not eligible for tax relief (except under the heavily circumscribed Business Expansion Scheme which, like all other schemes, denies relief to controlling owners of the business).

The benefits of these and other tax shelters have been diminished in the past decade by lower rates of taxation, and more recently by the less favourable treatment of capital gains for tax purposes, but they remain important and it is hardly surprising that the role of the private investor has decreased. Tax incentives channelling investment into financial institutions have historically been more generous in the UK than in other countries (for example, France does not provide tax relief for pension premia, while the US does not provide it for insurance premia) (Bannock 1990). This helps to explain why the direct ownership of shares is less important in the UK than elsewhere.

The tax system has not only stimulated the separation of ownership from control, and the channelling of savings into large takeover-prone firms; it has also encouraged smaller private companies to sell out to larger public ones and has favoured acquisition as against internal growth. This is a complex subject, but some of these other ways in which taxation favours acquisitions may be summarised briefly as follows. (Some of them are discussed in more detail in a paper by John Chown (1991) submitted to the Inquiry.)

- UK companies are obliged to 'impute' to shareholders tax at the standard rate on dividends and remit this to the Inland Revenue as advance corporation tax (ACT). ACT is then deductible from 'mainstream corporation tax'. Companies without sufficient taxable

UK profits to absorb ACT can either restrict their dividends, which may depress their share price and encourage a predator, or acquire more UK profits by acquisition.

- The acquirer may be able to offset profits and capital gains against losses incurred by the acquiree for corporation tax purposes, and may be able also to offset unrecoverable VAT liabilities. Scope for these reliefs has been restricted in recent years, however.

- Interest on borrowings for acquisitions (and other purposes) is deductible for corporation tax purposes.

- Private shareholders may prefer capital gains resulting from acquisitions to profits from internal growth , where capital gains are taxed more lightly than dividends. This factor is now less important than it was, and, for shareholders in the acquiree company, will depend upon the form of consideration (cash or shares on which gains can be rolled forward). In the past this factor encouraged controlling shareholders in private companies to sell out to quoted companies.

- Whilst the tax system favours acquisitions in these ways, it may discourage demergers except where the divestment remains as a separate entity in the hands of the original shareholders.

IV   Accounting and Disclosure

As mentioned in Chapter 1, acquisitions may be used to improve the apparent financial performance of the combined companies where no underlying improvement has actually taken place. Where this happens the enhanced performance may be reflected in the share price, which in turn may allow further acquisitions. Many observers believe that merger and accounting rules are too permissive in the way they allow post-merger performance to be reported.

Like taxation, accounting standards and practices for acquisitions is a complex subject which is beyond the scope of this Inquiry, though our view is that the issues raised are of less importance than the other matters dealt with in this chapter. The essential choice in accounting for acquisitions is between full consolidation and merger accounting. Under *full consolidation* or *acquisition accounting*, the acquirer includes the assets of its new subsidiary at their market value and writes off any premium paid for goodwill against earnings. Under *merger accounting* the assets of the acquiree are put into the balance sheet at historic cost, which presents a more favourable view, especially where the acquisition has been acquired by an exchange of shares.

Whatever accounting convention is used, acquisitions normally have a less unfavourable immediate effect upon the rate of return of the acquirer than the investment of similar resources in internal growth. New activities generally are carried out at a loss initially, since the investment has to be made before the returns come in, but provided the acquiree is profitable, these profits flow straight into the profit and loss statement without the increased depreciation provisions and write-offs that are usually associated with internal growth. Indeed, as mentioned, depending upon the relative balance sheet structures of the acquirer and acquiree, the rate of return on assets of the combined enterprise, as well as its gearing ratio and borrowing powers, may be enhanced immediately though the profitability of its component parts is unchanged.

In some highly geared acquisitions, however, a genuine increase in value added and returns on assets may be needed if the additional borrowing costs are to be serviced, though this may not be obvious from the accounts. Where this improvement is not, or cannot be achieved, then the survival of the enterprise will be threatened. There have been several examples of failures of this type recently.

Borrowings for acquisitions may, of course, be reduced by profitable asset sales after the event. Mr. Geoffrey Smith, who provided evidence to us, pointed out that many takeovers which have got into difficulties have been in industry sectors such as distributions, advertising and financial services. These types of businesses have relatively low created value as a percentage of sales and low created value per £ of pay. The major asset of these businesses is the skill, time, effort and know-how of employees and therefore cannot be converted into cash except through the created value process. Where the takeover has involved significant borrowings, then interest costs per £ of pay, when covered by debt interest to operating profit ratios, are near to or higher than the created value to pay ratios. This means there is insufficient cash being generated from creating value to sustain growth or repay loans. With created value to pay ratios at under 1:3, there is usually little room for manoeuvre. If employees leave or are made redundant to reduce costs, then the ability to create value to repay loans is reduced significantly. In these circumstances takeovers get into difficulty, since the major requirement for success-business growth is no longer a possibility.

It is interesting that these problems have not affected the large specialist conglomerates focussing on manufacturing, such as Hanson and BTR. Mr. Smith calculates, for example, that, in the period 1985–89, of the total increase in Hanson's pre-tax profits, 52 per cent can be traced to improved created value to pay and sales, 30 per cent to business growth and only 18 per cent to asset sales.

V Insider opportunities

Also important, though unquantifiable, as a force in favour of acquisitions are the benefits which accrue to the direct participants in the merger process and which may have little to do with the creation of real wealth. We have already shown that the acquiring management and the acquiree's shareholders may expect to gain in the merger process, but so too will market operators, arbitrageurs, issuing houses, advertising media, and professional advisers such as lawyers, accountants, management and PR consultants.

Morgan and Morgan (1990A) point out that the costs to bidding and target companies (other than management time) are revenues to the external advisers, suppliers and facilitators in the merger process. The higher these costs are, the greater the incentives 'for members of this group to seek out merger possibilities and to encourage companies to make and persist in bids'. It is not unusual for merchant banks and other advisers, with or without the encouragement of the predator, to attempt to bring potential merger parties together. In their investigations into the Rowntree case, Davis and Bannock (1991) identified one such attempt (not involving the ultimately successful bidder, Nestlé) five years before the company was actually put into play.

Market operators have a strong incentive to identify possible bid targets in the interests of greater trading volumes, and the analysts of broking houses frequently indulge in speculation of this kind. Speculation of a more practical kind is carried out by arbitrageurs (arbs) who purchase stakes in potential bid targets in the expectation of profit. Whilst stock exchange speculation may perform a useful economic function in general, in this case the acquisition of a significant stake by an arb may actually encourage a bid from elsewhere in the knowledge that this particular block of shares is available to a bidder.

Morgan and Morgan (1990A) point out that the burden of bid costs falls unequally and is not in any event borne by those who take the decisions. They state: '...Bidders are in a "no win, no fee" situation with regard to defenders' costs. If a bid succeeds, the winner usually, though not invariably, pays the loser's costs but, if it fails, the successful defender is left with all his own costs .... On whichever company the costs fall they are unlikely to fall personally on the directors and senior executives who influence decisions: the decision makers are seldom "playing with their own money".' We may add that the external adviser's fees are, of course, met whatever the outcome of the bid.

VI Countervailing forces

The pressures in favour of acquisitions are not all one way. The advantages of external over internal expansion; the decline of the owner-manager and the increase in institutional ownership; financial, taxation and accounting factors; and the vested interests in favour of merger activity, do not go unopposed.

Regulation has not in the UK, or in recent years in the US or elsewhere, appeared to be a very powerful force for restraining merger activity. In the period 1985–89, some 3,500 significant acquisitions of UK companies were recorded by the BSO. Of these, some 1,400 screened by the OFT had assets in excess of £30 million or qualified for investigation on the ground of the size of their market share.[1] However, only 50 of these qualifying mergers were actually referred for investigation and, as mentioned above, only 38 per cent were blocked or abandoned.

Of course it is possible that more larger merger bids would be made were it not for the prospect that they would be investigated and blocked by the authorities. Given that the scale of merger activity varies greatly between countries whereas the overall stringency of merger regulation, with a few exceptions, probably does not, it seems doubtful that regulation has been a major factor in determining the total level of this activity. Regulation may affect the type of mergers that take place, however. In the past, stringent controls over horizontal mergers in the US meant that few mergers of this type came before the authorities there (2 per cent of the total in 1979, compared with about 70 per cent in the UK), though the interpretation of US legislation has been less strict in recent years (Bannock 1990).

Attempted acquisitions are, of course, not without risk for the acquirer. As mentioned, some acquisitions have been disastrous for the successful bidder. In a hostile bid which fails, substantial costs will have been incurred to no purpose, and if it succeeds there may be skeletons in the cupboard. Post merger costs may be much higher than bargained for, key personnel may leave, and the expected synergistic benefits may prove to be illusory.

The strongest forces against the concentration of economic power are competition between unmerged business units and the entry of new businesses. If, through acquisition, companies become too large or overdiversified to be efficient, then we should expect them to lose out to smaller, more efficient companies or themselves to be taken over and broken up.

We saw in Chapter 2 that market forces have in fact stimulated a very large number of divestments by major companies in recent years, and there has also been a number of successful and unsuccessful bids made with the intention of breaking up diversified groups. Some of the largest of these bids have, paradoxically, been made by large conglomerates that virtually alone have access to the necessary financial and management resources to carry out this function.

---

[1]The OFT and BSO figures are not strictly comparable because the former include financial companies and acquisitions by non-UK companies as well as bids which were unsuccessful.

PART II: ANALYSIS

4 Takeovers and Economic Performance

I Introduction

In Part I of this Report, attention was concentrated on a description of the takeover process. Part I confirmed certain features of the takeover process which have been frequently noted, but it also drew attention to several features which are less familiar and which were derived from the research commissioned by the Inquiry itself. It will be noted that most of those less familiar features concentrate on the activities of 'market makers' who have a strong interest in maximising their incomes from the takeover process.

In Part II of the Report, an evaluation of takeovers is undertaken which considers the public interest. This process of evaluation is vital before considering any policy recommendations which are considered in Part III.

In identifying what 'the public interest' means, no attempt has been made to specify what economists would term a 'social welfare function', often presented in professional literature in very formal terms (for an example see, Blaug 1980). 'Social welfare' is usually defined fairly narrowly by economists and is assumed to be a function only of economic efficiency and possibly some distributional aim, though other aims of society may be promoted by 'maximising the function'. In any case, the specification of such a function is a matter of considerable controversy amongst economists themselves (see Rowley and Peacock, 1975). It is more in keeping with the purpose of this Report to identify the aspects of corporate takeovers which appear to be matters of public concern.

Three such matters are identified in this Report:

i)   the effect of corporate takeovers on the performance of the British economy;

ii) their effect on the distribution of economic power between different national economies and within the British economy;

iii) the issues raised by takeover activity concerning the ethics of business behaviour.

Before proceeding to consider each matter in detail, some preliminary discussion of our approach to these matters may be helpful.

Firstly, we make no attempt to assign any order of priority in identifying the nexus between takeover activity and aims of society implicit in these concerns. It is left to the reader to rank the aims or how to 'trade them off' against one another.

Secondly, while any conclusions reached may have to rely to a large extent on the judgment of the rapporteurs, the basis of such judgment varies from one matter to another. The evaluation of the effects of takeover activity on economic performance has been intensively investigated and, as Part I shows, there is a mass of empirical evidence, including our own, which requires digestion. In contrast, the evaluation of the ethical issues raised by takeovers is beset by the difficulties encountered in defining what is 'proper behaviour'. Thus, while it is likely that a definition of 'economic performance' and how it may be measured can be broadly agreed upon, it may be too much to expect that a consensus can be arrived at concerning norms of behaviour.

Thirdly, the three matters of concern are closely connected with each other. For example, it is argued (see Elliot, HOP 14) that the improvement in the overall performance of the British economy itself depends on the dissemination of economic power so that judgment of takeovers with regard to matter (i) cannot be separated from matter (ii). To take another example; the working of any market economy must rest on principles of behaviour, such as abiding by contracts, both explicit and implicit, not all of which have the force of law – as instanced in the Takeover Code (see Manser, HOP 21). All that need to be said at this stage is that exploration of these interconnexions, while not a major feature of the Report, needs to be made.

Fourthly, the terms of reference of the Inquiry require that particular attention is paid to the Rowntree/Nestlé takeover (see Davis and Bannock, HOP 30). It would be foolish to base any generalisation about the effects of takeovers on one case. Indeed, there are important respects in which this takeover may not be typical. Nevertheless, all the major issues about the effects of takeover were raised by this case, as it was perceived by those directly affected by it. This alone makes it both interesting and informative.

II Meaning of Economic Performance

Economic performance may be given a general meaning, namely the rate of economic growth as measured by Gross Domestic (or National) Product by itself or per head. There are, of course, other measures of economic performance such as the growth in employment, the rate of unemployment and the inflation rate, but the rate of economic growth is usually singled out because corporate takeovers are discerned as having some effect on the growth performance of individual companies whose net output is a component of GDP. Thus the Office of Fair Trading (HOP 18, p.17) contends that the object of mergers policy is "to strengthen the forces making for industrial and commercial efficiency and growth". Many similar statements could be identified in both official and unofficial discussion of the takeover phenomenon.

Assuming that it is possible to trace the connexion between the incidence of takeovers and economic performance – and there are analytical difficulties to be faced in doing so – some form of comparison is implied. Within a particular economy, one might compare different periods of time in which the incidence of takeovers were different and relate them in some way to the rate of economic growth. This is not an exercise which excites much interest and there would be technical obstacles in performing it such as the absence of comparable data over long periods of time. Contemporary interest is centred more directly in comparisons with other advanced economies, and this Inquiry follows suit. Whether such comparisons offer conclusive evidence of the relation between the incidence of takeovers and economic growth is a matter for further investigation.

Economic performance is usually given a specific if not more precise meaning in contemporary discussion of the effects of takeovers. While it is assumed that the ultimate aim of interest is economic performance in the general sense already described, the proximate meaning of 'performance' is the contribution of takeovers and mergers to economic efficiency and by implication the effect of changes in industrial structure on the main spur to efficiency – competition. As put in evidence to us by the Department of Trade and Industry (HOP 18, p.28), "(c)ompetition in free markets leads to an efficient, productive and flexible economy, which both delivers to consumers the goods and services they require at the lowest possible prices, and forms the only lasting basis for secure employment. In short, competition is good for wealth creation."

Performance is now being judged by the contribution of industry to achieving an allocation of resources in line with consumer choices and not simply by the growth in the total amount of goods and services. It will be noted, however, that the DTI statement embraces the suggestion that competition will also expand consumer opportunities by improving growth prospects.

The Report takes it as axiomatic that competition will have these effects, generally perceived as desirable, on allocation and growth performance, though fully aware that consumer preferences may not be fully met by market decisions alone. This enables the Report to concentrate on the relation between takeover activity and the promotion of competition, particularly in the capital market.

III   Corporate Takeovers and the Capital Market

If consumers are to derive the maximum benefit from allocating their income, then producers of goods and services must supply goods at minimum prices and maximum quality subject to earning at least enough profit to offer an incentive to remain in business. However, it is the prospect that the company may make "super-normal" profits which spurs its owners to find ways of maximising the difference between revenue and costs and to grow. Such opportunities may arise because a company adjusts more quickly to a change in consumer tastes than its rivals, or because it invents a new product which catches the fancy of the public. In these cases, the pursuit of profit accords with the object of consumer sovereignty provided that competition is not destroyed in the process. Put in modern jargon, the market must be 'contestable', with rival firms and potential entrants in a position to compete on price and quality. Monopoly gains, provided they are short-run, perform an important function in promoting the dynamic adjustment of supply to changes in demand. At the same time, monopoly gains derived from suppressing competition clearly inhibits the dynamic adjustment process and are against the interests of the consumer.

Whether monopoly gains are derived from seeking out market opportunities or by suppressing competition, their pursuit involves companies in constant examination of their corporate structure. The achievement of profit targets may be judged by a company to entail adding to its capital stock and a frequent method for doing so is that of corporate takeover involving a change in ownership of assets. In UK and USA, finance for capital investment is usually derived from retained earnings, the issue of securities which are actively traded on stock exchanges or by bank borrowing. Hence a judgement on whether corporate takeovers promote efficiency in the use of resources depends on the view taken of the efficiency of the capital market itself.

The evidence received from government departments and the OFT (see HOP 18) indicates that they take a relaxed view of the way in which the capital market facilitates the transfer in the ownership of assets by merger and takeover, including 'hostile bids'. The capital market is by implication 'efficient', except in one important respect, namely that it cannot prevent a situation where merger or takeover suppresses competition in goods and services supplied to the final consumer, and hence may lead to monopoly profits which do not promote the interests of the consumer. The DTI state (HOP 18, p.29) that "the Government should only intervene in those mergers in which the private interests and the public interests diverge – typically where a merger has the potential to allow the abuse of the merged enterprise's monopoly power. The Government does not believe that it would be consistent with this general approach to intervene more generally in mergers, for whatever reason." This view, commonly referred to as the 'Tebbit philosophy', echoes those of prominent financial economists on both sides of the Atlantic who have buttressed them with both sophisticated economic modelling and large-scale empirical investigation, though they have recently been placed more on the defensive (for details see Gowland (HOP 20), Reid (HOP 22) and Morgan (HOP 24)).

It is beyond the scope of this Report to offer a full exposition of the economic modelling of the capital market, though the interested reader will find ample material for study in the Research Papers just referred to. Presumably what is behind the thinking of the Government and of others who take a benign view of takeovers is that an efficient capital market would operate so as to select the most profitable investment opportunities. In such a market, only those takeovers would succeed which would improve the profitability of the companies involved.

Whether or not this last proposition will hold can be investigated in two ways. The first is to examine the capital market and see if its structure conforms with that assumed in the financial model underlying it. The second is to consider how far empirical evidence supports the predictions of the model itself, in regard to takeover activity.

IV   The Efficient Market Hypothesis and the Market for Corporate Control

An authoritative version of the efficient market hypothesis (efmh) can be derived from the analysis of James Tobin, the Nobel Laureate in Economics (see Tobin, 'On the Efficiency of the Financial System', *Lloyds Annual Bank Review*, vol. 2, 1989, edited by Christopher Johnson). To quote Tobin,

> First, a market is 'efficient' if it is on average impossible to gain from trading on the basis of generally available public information. In efficient markets, only insiders can make money, consistently anyway. Whatever you and I know the market has already 'discounted'. The revealing standard anecdote goes like this: "Finance professor is walking on campus with his research assistant, who says 'Professor, I see a twenty dollar bill on the sidewalk. Should I pick it up?'. 'No, of course not, if it were really there, it would have already been picked up'. Efficiency in this meaning I call *information–arbitrage efficient*.

The implication of this view is that share prices will adjust swiftly to market information to reflect the effects of the news on current market value. A record of share price movements would present a random series of observations which is why this version of the theory has been labelled the 'random walk hypothesis'. It would also follow that if adjustments to new information are rapid, investors should be highly sceptical of brokers' recommendations and professionally managed funds should not be able to outperform the market.

It is clearly relevant to shareholders examining the virtues of a merger or takeover bid to have full information. Both acquiring companies and their targets will have an incentive to supply it, but whether it will be the whole truth is an open question to be examined later. The more competitive the market, the more likely will be the incentive to supply full information. In any case, long-established markets such as the securities market have evolved rules about information provision which presumably would not have been accepted if those operating in the market did not think it was to their general advantage. Generally speaking, such rules require that information from companies about changes in their circumstances should be announced in such a way that it becomes readily available to all.

This Report does not consider the empirical evidence for this view of stock market efficiency, other than to say that it supports the view that securities markets tend to be 'information-arbitrage efficient' (see Tobin, *op.cit.* and Morgan (HOP 24) but notes the reservations of Reid in HOP 22). However, quick adjustment of the securities market to information does not by itself determine the market's capacity for identifyng those takeovers or mergers which promote economic efficiency as already defined (see Section I of this Chapter). All that the random walk hypothesis tells us is that reactions to information will result in quick adjustments of prices. That may be a technical achievement but it does not guarantee that the information supplied is comprehensive, accurate and relevant. Nor does it guarantee that the information will be interpreted correctly so that stockholders know whether the valuations of the stock of companies involved in takeover conform with their financial prospects.

The very idea of an efficient market presupposes that it works in such a way as to maximise the satisfaction of the 'consumers', in the case of the capital market the buyers and therefore the owners of the share capital of companies. The buying and selling of shares consequent on a merger or takeover would be judged by how far it reflects the preferences of the owners of capital. The second version of the efficient market hypothesis is more relevant to our Inquiry because it offers an analysis of the motivation of those who buy and sell shares and what would constitute a situation where the capital market reflects the valuation of assets by shareholders. 'Fundamental valuation efficiency' to use Tobin's term (Tobin *op.cit.* and Morgan, HOP 24) is achieved if the valuation of a financial asset 'reflects' accurately the future payments to which the asset gives title – to use currently fashionable jargon, if the price of the asset is based on 'rational expectations' of these payments (Tobin, *op.cit.* p.126).

The basic assumption in the model – there are many versions (see Reid, HOP 22) – is that investors in the stock market seek to maximize financial gains. However, assets have various degrees of risk attached to them and, as is commonly assumed, investors are risk-averse, they will wish to spread their risks, to achieve an optimal balance between risk and return. This calls for a diversified portfolio. The investor may be regarded as diversifying his portfolio with reference to some risk-free asset. The actions of investors taken together would produce a situation where the *expected* market rate of return on a risky asset is equal to the rate on the risk-free asset plus a risk premium. Investors can obtain statistical estimates of the riskiness of the market in the past on which to form their expectations. The risk premium is known in the trade as the Beta coefficient which compares the risk of the asset with the riskiness of the market as a whole. Thus if for a particular asset $B=1$, then it has the same riskiness as the market. A fall in the market rate of return by 5 per cent would be complemented by a fall of 5 per cent in that of the asset in question. If $B<1$, then a rise in the return on the asset would be less than that for any rise in the market rate of return. (For detailed analysis, see Reid, HOP 22.)

The test of efficiency arises when there is some change in market circumstances which affects either the degree of riskiness or the market rate of return and therefore causes investors to alter their portfolios in order to achieve an optimal balance. Efficiency would require a quick adjustment to any such new situation reflecting the market's revised view of the profitability of companies. If takeovers are a major feature when such changes take place, the stock market becomes not only a mechanism for the buying and selling of shares of existing companies but a market for corporate control. Thus the expectation that a takeover 'raider' may well be able to put the assets of the target company to better use must imply that the takeover would raise profitability and capital value. It is this expectation that gives rise to a controversial statement such as this: "The market for corporate control is creating large benefits for shareholders for the economy as a whole by loosening control over vast amounts of resources and enabling them to move more quickly to their highest-valued use. This is a healthy market in operation, on both the takeover side and the divestiture side, and it is playing an important role in helping the American economy adjust to major changes in competition and regulation of the past decade." (Jensen, 1988.)

Before examining the evidence which would throw light on the proposition that the market for corporate control works in such a way as to maximise the wealth of shareholders and benefits society as a whole, it is important to examine the underlying assumptions of the hypothesis.

The first is that, even if the motivation of wealth holders is to maximise the expected value of their assets, the uncertainty surrounding future earnings means making predictions which pick out the variables which will affect these earnings and assign them values. Information on the past, including Beta co-efficients, may offer a suitable point of departure for analysis of future trends. However, the variables which will affect a company's profitability may change through time and not in a systematic way and their inter-relations may be complex and varied. Putting values to the variables involves making a whole range of strong assumptions. Turning this information into estimates of the future profitability of any individual company will be very difficult and the range of estimates between seasoned predictors may be wide. Some 'strong' versions of the efficient market hypothesis adopt the assumption that investors' expectations are consistent with each other, as for example, if investors make identical estimates of the expected distribution of returns from companies. Given the range of estimates facing them, this assumption is clearly untenable, though it might still be argued that when investors get it wrong, they may be able to act quickly in a market where buying and selling afford quick adjustment of portfolios. The fact remains that if such large variations are possible in long-term valuations of expected profitability, the guidance offered to shareholders on the profitability of takeovers could be of very limited value, even if those who supply the information have no vested interest in influencing shareholders' decisions.

This last observation draws attention to the second feature of the capital market, calling fundamental valuation efficiency in question. Consider the contrast between the process of decision making by an individual in respect of buying goods and buying shares. An individual buying bottles of beer acquires very quickly a knowledge of the satisfaction to be derived from beer because he can buy it round the corner, can regularly test the product and can switch his custom easily from one beer to another. If he buys shares, he is buying claims to the assets of a company which he may never see and not even recognize if he saw them. He is not likely to have direct knowledge of the link between the productivity of the asset and its effect on sales and profits. Acquiring the information himself typically involves high costs in relation to the proposed investment in claims, particularly the specialised knowledge of alternative investment opportunities. It therefore seems sensible for an investor to seek the services of those who can reduce these costs to a minimum, services for which he must be prepared to pay directly or indirectly. It is for this reason that, investors, in Britain at least, rely not only on the advice of brokers but also on investment and unit trusts that not only digest the information for him but advise on the structure of his portfolio in return for a fee. If a condition of employment is that the individual must take out a personal pension or join an occupational pension scheme, then he is bound to leave to others the day-to-day investment decisions which are designed to secure his pension rights. Furthermore, whether or not he holds his own portfolio or assigns this task to others, he has to assume that the management of the companies is conducted in such a way as to maximise the value of his claims, or that, if this is not the case, companies will have an incentive to replace inefficient managers.

Even the most resolute defenders of the efficient market hypothesis would admit that the attenuated link between shareholders and the assets to which they lay claim creates what is called in the trade 'an agency problem'. The owners of capital, the shareholders, may be termed the 'principals' in a transaction with 'agents' – managers of their shareholdings, and controllers of the assets to which they lay claim – who, if the theory is correct, will have sufficient incentives to comply with their wishes. Adam Smith may have supported their case by arguing that 'the private interests and passions of men naturally lead them to divide and distribute the stock of every society .....as nearly as possible in the proportion which is most agreeable to the interest of the whole society', but he had in mind those who risked their own capital. He offered the warning that those who are managing other people's money have not the same incentive to exercise the 'anxious vigilance' which they do over their own. Notwithstanding this admission that agency problems may arise in creating an efficient capital market, influential writers in the US, such as Manne and Jensen (see Reid, HOP 22, pp.24–25), have argued that a 'takeover market' is a mechanism for reducing agency costs to a minimum. According to them, a market in shares which facilitates the transfer of assets through the buying and selling of companies will act as an effective discipline on managers of companies threatened by takeover. If managers wish to retain control of their companies, and therefore keep their jobs, then they must seek to maximise the return on the company's assets. The threat of competition from outside should produce a strong positive association between the share price and managerial efficiency. There is an echo of this view in the DTI evidence to the Inquiry (HOP 18, p.29); .... "the threat of takeover does appear to have a salutary effect on the incumbent managements of public companies. Any government action which places obstacles in the way of takeovers weakens this discipline." Clearly, this proposition requires further investigation and this Report returns to the subject in order to do so.

It is significant that the discussion of the agency problem in the US literature is illustrated mainly by potential conflicts of interest between managers of companies and their owners, the shareholders. However, the proportion of shares directly held by private shareholders in the USA is twice as high as it is in the UK. This fact draws attention to a third feature of the capital market in Britain, namely the effect on the market of the domination of large institutional investors acting on behalf of individual savers. This raises doubts about the extent to which share prices in bidding operations meet the requirements of a competitive market in which there is a large volume of continuous trading between a large number of buyers and sellers. The market for corporate control could be markedly influenced by the view taken by the institutions of the bids for shares made by companies seeking to acquire other companies.

It is with these doubts and reservations in mind about the strength of the efficient market hypothesis (efmh) that we turn to examine the evidence on which a judgment about the economic performance of takeovers must be based.

V   Corporate Takeovers and Economic Performance: the Equity Market

If an efficient capital market operates to select the most profitable investment opportunities, then a criterion emerges for judging mergers and takeovers: the earnings subsequent to merger or takeover would be consistent with the expectations embodied in the share prices at the time of merger or takeover. The problem is how to devise suitable tests for deciding whether or not this criterion has been met.

The first test which might be used is a very simple one. If share prices accurately reflected a company's rationally expected future earnings, bidders would have to be prepared to pay a premium if they expected a merger to raise earnings. At the same time, there would be no reason to suppose that that premium should be other than small in relation to the prevailing market price, given alternative opportunities open to investors. The Morgans (HOP 24) have analysed the average premiums as a percentage of share prices one day and one month before offer over recent years. In 1989, for example, premiums averaged 29 per cent over the price running on the day before the offer and 37 per cent above the price a month before. They quote as examples of large premiums the BA bid for British Caledonian which, once it was cleared with the Monopolies and Mergers Commission (MMC), rose from 147 pence to eventually 250 pence, and an original offer of 22.8 pence for Dunlop which was raised nearly three-fold to 66 pence. These results hardly suggest that the stock market reflected the underlying profitability of the companies concerned but rather the 'agency problem' referred to above.

The second test used is to compare post-merger with pre-merger performance, implying that it was generally expected that, as a result of merger, subsequent earnings of the merged companies would line up with the share prices at the time of takeover. There is a problem about using such a test. It implies that if post-merger earnings were less than expected, then the only reason for this must be that the market was influenced by something which could not have been foreseen. This assumes what has to be proved, namely that investors behave in the first place exactly as 'efmh' would predict. It would be consistent with the post-merger facts if it were argued that a company's actual differed from its expected performance because the market is imperfect, e.g. the information available at the time that expectations were formed was limited, or because investors' behaved in a very different way from that which 'rational expectations' theory suggests. Indeed, it has become fashionable to divide investors into the 'smart money' operators and ordinary investors, referred to as 'noise traders'. The former behave more or less in line with 'efmh' and the latter regard the cost of 'research' into share values as exceeding the benefits derived from following market fads and fashions. (In old-fashioned jargon, they were known as 'dabbling outsiders'.) In the formation of market opinion by analysts and commentators, there can be "no means of distinguishing between prices that reflect rational expectations of future earnings and those that do not, so that prices that are 'wrong' are unlikely to be corrected by arbitrage dealing" (Morgan HOP 24, p.74). The lack of efficiency reflected in bid premiums already referred to is consistent with the view that the best informed view of future dividend streams (the 'smart money') does not dominate share prices.

Whatever model of investment behaviour is being tested, some assessment of post-merger performance is important if we are to be able to approach an answer to the problem of deciding whether or not corporate takeovers provide economic benefits. An examination of the testing methods used should help the Inquiry.

An earlier approach by Newbould (1970), which preceded the date when much more statistical information became available, relied on in-depth interviews with managers of merged companies. Newbould's pioneering work consisted of 38 case studies. He found that 2 years after the completion of a merger, half of the merged companies claimed to be pleased with the result, leaving half who could not identify any positive benefit, of which half of this group described the merger as a failure. This method has the merit that it is based on the actual perceptions of those running companies, but it is bound to be impressionistic.

A rash of detailed studies on an assessment of company performance based on the accounting rate of return on capital employed (ARR). (For detailed information, see Morgan HOP 24, Part V., Gowland, HOP 20, p.3.) This assessment has two components: (i) comparison of the combined rate (ARR) of the 'unmerged' companies over a pre-merger period with a consolidated rate over a post-merger period; (ii) a comparison between merged and non-merged companies over the same period in order to eliminate economic factors which would affect general profitability.

There are some awkward problems encountered in using accounting data, mainly concerned with the bias introduced into the calculation of ARR by the treatment of the profits of acquired companies in the year of merger and the valuation of 'goodwill' in the consolidated merger accounts. These need at least passing mention. Assuming that these problems can be resolved satisfactorily, care has to be taken in arriving at the choice of a period of comparison and of a control group. Ideally, the merger sample should comprise companies that have made only one merger during the period, whereas the control group should contain no companies undertaking mergers. An attempt must be made to match the sample of merged companies in respect of the size of companies and the particular industrial category into which they fall. The period of time must clearly be long enough to avoid the possibility that random influences will distort the comparison. These are rigid requirements when, as at present, takeovers are so frequent.

The Morgan study (HOP 24) offers a useful summary of the results of studies following these methods of comparison and one can do no better than to quote it *in extenso*:

> Considering differences in the periods covered and the ways of tackling the problems outlined above, the general results of the studies we have surveyed show a surprising degree of unanimity. The results are:
>
> A majority of companies in the mergers sample showed a decline in profitability, relative to the control group, in the post-merger period, but a substantial minority (in one case as large as 48 per cent) showed an improvement; and
> Average profitability relative to the control group declined though the decline was generally small and, in some cases, not statistically significant.

> Three interesting qualifications to these general results have been found. Meeks (1977) and Cosh, Hughes and Singh (1980) found a difference between horizontal and non-horizontal mergers. For horizontal mergers, however, both found small but significant improvements. A possible explanation suggested by Hughes is that acquiring firms in non-horizontal mergers had a better pre-merger profits record than those in horizontal mergers in both samples; this may have signified superior management, the merits of which were carried over to the merged group. (Hughes 1989.)
> In one study (Cosh, Hughes, Kumar, and Singh 1985) the authors split their sample into cases where the acquiring companies had a large institutional shareholding and others. Those with relatively small institutional holdings conformed to the general pattern established by other studies – a small

decline in post-merger performance. Those with large institutional holdings showed a small improvement in profitability, though this was not statistically significant.

Finally, in another study (Hall and Pickering, 1986), the authors examined the performance of companies involved in failed mergers as well as in completed ones. They compared matched samples of 50 successful and 50 failed bids. The successful sample showed the usual preponderance of companies with falling post-merger profitability, but there was a widespread improvement in performance among both bidding and target companies in the 'failed' sample. The authors conclude that this is evidence of the disciplinary role of the market in improving the efficiency of management, though the conclusion seems rather dubious.

To sum up, accounting studies of profitability have provided very little help in assessing the performance of mergers in relation to the public interest. In view of the conceptual and practical problems outlined at the beginning of this section, a strong conclusion one way or the other would be needed in order to carry much conviction. In fact, the conclusions of these studies could hardly be weaker. Mergers appear to have very little effect either way on profitability and such effect as they do have is, more often than not, harmful. The findings on non-horizontal mergers, on holdings by financial institutions, and on failed bids are interesting but they need a lot more support from other work if they are to become more than 'straws in the wind'.

The third test looks more hopeful than the second (ARR) test which uses accounting information open to different interpretations. It consists in examining data on changes in shareholder wealth as a result of takeovers, so concentrating on the perceived benefits from the investor's point of view. The changes in shareholder wealth are represented by dividends (which are assumed to be reinvested) and the change in share prices over a given period. Major studies have been undertaken which compare the returns to shareholders in a sample of merged companies with a matching control group of companies in which mergers did not occur or with the market as a whole.

The studies undertaken using this third test cannot simply assume that the only circumstances peculiar to any company as compared with the market as a whole will be the incidence of takeover. Whether or not a takeover occurs, the valuation placed on the shares of an individual company will depend on the market's view of the risk attached to investing in that company. As explained earlier, the Beta co-efficient is a way of attaching a measure of the sensitivity of an individual company to market fluctuations. In order to take account of this risk factor it is the practice in applying this third test to compare the returns for the market as a whole not with the actual return on the shares of a particular company but with a 'normalised' return by multiplying it by the company's 'beta value', the so-called Market Model. This normalised return can then be compared with the market and the returns are cumulated over the period of comparison. If the cumulative normalised return is greater than the market return then this is taken as an indicator of the success of a merger.

The Inquiry commissioned Professor and Mrs. Morgan to examine the evidence for an abnormal return (AR) as defined, and again it is appropriate to quote their conclusions:

By far the largest study of this kind using UK data is by Franks and Harris (1986). They examined nearly 1,900 mergers that occurred in the 30 years 1955–85. They found very substantial abnormal returns to shareholders in target companies. Over a period beginning 4 months before a bid these averaged 30 per cent with 85 per cent of the sample showing a positive AR. Some of the benefits of a bid were apparently discounted by the market in the run-up period, but there was still an average AR of 22 per cent in the bid month.

Positive ARs for bidding companies in the bid month averaged only 1 per cent and accrued to only half the sample. Over a period of 6 months, beginning 4 months before the bid, ARs averaged 7 per cent and accrued to 65 per cent of companies. The authors point out that part at least of these gains may have arisen not from the market's anticipation of the bids, but because managers tend to make bids when their shares are highly valued for other reasons. A study of post-merger performance over 2 years shows that acquiring companies performed slightly better than the market as a whole but less well than they, themselves, had done before the merger. In a subsequent publication, the authors describe their work as showing 'positive gains to shareholders in merging firms with most if not all of the gain going to acquiree shareholders' (in Fairburn & King, 1989, p.158).

No-one has questioned the finding that shareholders in acquired companies make large gains from mergers. Indeed, some studies find these gains to be even more widespread than do Franks and Harris. One major study of 434 mergers found positive ARs in no less than 431 cases (Firth, 1980).

There is less unanimity as to the effect on acquiring companies. Franks and Harris found a small positive effect in the month of the merger, but Firth and others have found negative ones. Firth found net abnormal losses for 350 of his 434 cases. There is widespread agreement, however, that post-merger performance tends to deteriorate, relatively to the market over a period of up to 2 years following an acquisition.

Since acquiring companies are usually much larger than targets, a large percentage gain by acquirees can be offset by a small percentage loss by acquirers. Franks and Harris found net gains in the short run, while Firth found net losses.

The evidence can be summarised as follows:

Mergers usually produce large abnormal returns to shareholders in target companies both in the run-up to a bid and at the time of the announcement.

This is particularly so in the case of contested and revised bids.

Positive abnormal returns to shareholders in bidding companies are often found in the few months prior to a bid, but these may be due to other circumstances.

Abnormal returns to bidding companies in the month of an announcement are usually small and it is uncertain whether gains or losses predominate.

Post-merger performance of acquiring companies tends to deteriorate relatively to the market over a period of up to 2 years from an acquisition.

The net effect of mergers on shareholder wealth is uncertain and probably
small. There is a balance of evidence that abnormal gains are positive in the
short run, though this is far from conclusive. It is fairly certain that net gains
decline over time and, in the longer run, they may well be negative.

Studies using stock market data provide little evidence that mergers, at
least in the UK, have significant effects in either direction on shareholders'
wealth. Moreover, even if a positive wealth effect could be established it
tells us very little about the relationship between mergers and the public
interest. If the stock market were fundamental valuation efficient, a positive wealth effect would indicate an improvement in rationally expected
profitability of the real capital assets owned by the merging companies
and subject to the qualifications this could be accepted as in the public
interest. However, there are strong *a priori* reasons for believing that
the market is not efficient in this sense, and this belief is supported by
the size of premiums and the frequency with which bids are revised.
(HOP 24, pp.79–81.)

VI   Corporate Takeovers and Economic Performance: Testing the 'Managerial' Hypothesis

Reference was made in Section III of this chapter to the 'agency problem'
which suggests that the motive for takeovers should be closely associated
with the interests of managers of companies. In Part I, the Report placed
particular emphasis on the various techniques used by managers of companies under threat of takeover to beat off predators, although 'efmh' would
claim that the stock market acts as a rigorous disciplinarian in directing
managerial skills towards maximizing the return on a company's assets.
In a spirited defence of this view which deserves close scrutiny, Jensen
(1988) emphasised this point:

....when the internal processes of change in large corporations are too slow,
costly, and clumsy to bring about the restructuring or change in managers
efficiently, the capital markets, through the market for corporate control are
doing so. The takeover market serves as an important source of protection
for investors in these situations. Other management teams that recognize an
opportunity to reorganise or redeploy an organization's assets and thereby
create new value can bid for control rights in the takeover market. To be
successful, such bids must give investors an opportunity to realize part of the
gains from reorganization and redeployment of assets (p.28).

There is at least a realization in the 'efmh' that there can be a conflict
of interest between managers and shareholders. Equally, those who have
emphasized the importance of managerial behaviour as the major factor

determining the structure and development of the allocation of capital have not denied that managerial objectives will be constrained by the ability of those who supply capital to switch investments. On the contrary, managerial objectives will certainly support takeovers, provided that these improve their economic prospects.

An elaboration of this point suggests another way for testing the efficiency of takeover. Instead of postulating that managers act in accordance with the interests of shareholders, let it be assumed that they only do so if this accords with their own economic prospects. Shareholders are in a weak position when it comes to 'monitoring the monitors' – the managers of the company. The strong version of this thesis postulates that managers see the way to improve their prospects largely through more rapid growth in the company than is warranted by shareholders' objectives, and this objective would be achieved more easily by acquisition of other companies than by internal expansion. Support for this hypothesis could be found if shareholders of rapidly growing firms were to obtain inferior returns from acquisitions than their counterparts in less rapidly growing firms. An extension of this hypothesis suggests that managers would wish to pursue a diversified acquisitions strategy, i.e. takeover of unrelated products or services, as their way of reducing risk of failure to grow. This would clearly be against the shareholders' interests, which would be to seek extra returns, provided that they could achieve risk reduction by holding a well diversified portfolio. Support for this extension of the hypothesis would lie in evidence that related mergers achieve a higher level of post-acquisition performance than unrelated mergers.

Robin Limmack of Stirling University has made a special study of the link between managerial theories of the firm and corporate takeovers which throws light on these hypotheses. A fuller account of his methodology and results is to be found in Limmack (HOP 19) and only an outline of both is given here.

He had, first of all, to identify those wealth changes in companies which are related to takeover bids, so that it is necessary to eliminate those market-wide movements in security prices of a general nature. He uses a variant of the Market Model explained in the previous section which controls for the risk of individual securities, and which corrects for a downward bias found in calculations of post-acquisition returns to shareholders of bidder companies. The calculation of bid company returns covered a period from the beginning of the bid month to 24 months following the month of announcement of the bid outcome.

He needed, secondly, a measure of company growth and chose two: the growth in capital employed pre- and post-acquisition and growth in trading income.

Thirdly, he needed a measure of profitability and used two versions of the return on capital employed (ROCE), the average ROCE and the increase in ROCE, where ROCE is defined as pre-tax profit before interest is deducted divided by total capital employed, excluding intangibles, plus borrowings repayable within one year.

Finally, he had to find some way of identifying whether mergers of companies covered related or unrelated activities. He first of all classified the areas of activity of both bidder and target for the year prior to acquisition and then, on a judgmental basis, classified each bid according to whether the merger was horizontal, vertical or conglomerate.

Mr. Limmack's statistical analysis, using multi-regression analysis, must be of considerable interest to specialists, but only the conclusions of particular relevance to this Inquiry are given:

i)   He found a significant negative relationship between the growth of bidding firms and the returns obtained from acquired companies. This would offer support to the hypothesis that 'bad' acquisitions are indeed related to the pursuit of managerial objectives.

ii) He found no evidence that the returns derived from acquisitions are a function of the degree of diversification through mergers.

Mr. Limmack added a coda to his conclusions of some importance. He analysed the pattern of returns for two separate time periods – 1977–80 and 1981–86 – and found:

> a significant difference in the pattern of returns between the two sub-periods. The change in economic climate and regulatory framework appears to have led to an improvement in the efficiency of operations of the market for corporate control in the United Kingdom. There does also appear to be some as yet undetected relationship between the health of the economy and returns from acquisitions. Finally, the results obtained should provide a warning against reading too much into the findings of studies into security price behaviour using data extracted from relatively short time periods.

VII   Corporate Takeovers and Overall Economic Performance

(a)   Differences in Overall Performance

The discussion of the effects of corporate takeovers on economic performance so far has concentrated on evidence designed to test analytical propositions concerning the capital market as a market in corporate control. Any consideration of the policy implications of takeover activities has to address the question of the relation between the degree of takeover activity and the *magnitude* of its effect. This is usually done by considering whether or not takeovers affect the rate of investment and particularly new capital formation and, consequently, the rate of economic growth. Further, judgment of overall economic performance, as already indicated, entails a discussion of the comparative economic performance of large industrialised countries, such as Germany, Japan, the USA and the UK.

The basic facts regarding comparative performance of these economies are well known, but bear repeating here. Table 4.1 offers a bald summary of them:

Table 4.1 INVESTMENT, GROWTH IN GDP PER HEAD AND
TAKEOVER ACTIVITY, SELECTED COUNTRIES

Country	Gross Fixed Capital Formation (% GDP)		Percentage Growth in GDP/Head Annual Average 1960–1989	Recent Incidence of takeovers
	1960	1989		
Italy	22.6	20.2	3.5	Low
Germany	24.3	20.7	2.7[2]	Low
France	20.1	20.8	3.1	Intermediate
Japan	29.8[1]	31.2[2]	5.5[2]	Low
USA	17.9	16.5	2.1[2]	High
UK	16.4	19.5	2.1	High

SOURCE   International Financial Statistics, Yearbook 1990, IMF
NOTE   1 1965; 2 GNP not GDP

There are many ways in which this table might be extended, by time period, by countries, by supplementary indicators, but the Inquiry has not come across any major disagreements about the conclusions that they suggest:

i)   the rates of capital formation in Germany Italy, France and Japan have been considerably higher than in the USA and UK;

ii) the rates of economic growth have been higher in Germany Italy, France and Japan than in the UK and USA;

iii) the incidence of corporate takeover in Germany and Japan is small compared with the USA and UK.

This last conclusion requires further elaboration. There is a wealth of information which throws light on the reasons why takeover activity is much lower in Japan, Germany and other non-Anglo-Saxon countries (for bibliography, see IPPR, Industrial Policy Paper No.3, Takeovers and Short-Termism in the UK, by Cosh *et al*, 1990). The points which are normally highlighted are:

i)   the importance of the legal constitution of companies in Germany which gives workers' representation on Boards of supervision and management;

ii) the importance of lifetime employment in Japanese firms which inhibits any form of takeover which would entail dismissal of workers;

iii) the relatively small size of the stock markets in Germany, Italy and France;

iv) the close relationships between German companies and banks offering loan finance, with banks more concerned with long-term performance than with share price movements;

v) the non-existence in Japan and Germany of stock options as a method of remunerating management, and therefore no link between share prices and managerial rewards.

There are obvious pitfalls in interpreting these data, but we can safely say that the strong hypothesis that corporate takeovers are a necessary condition for a 'satisfactory' economic performance is not borne out by what we know of economic relationships of the immediate past. Nor do the data 'prove' that takeovers inhibit economic performance, for there could be so many other factors which could explain the variation in performance between the different countries. However, there are convincing explanations of the data which are consistent with what we know about the investment process in these countries. The most important of these concentrates on the phenomenon of 'short-termism' as the factor governing investment decisions in the UK.

(b) 'Short-Termism'

Short-termism is usually explained as a conflict between those who supply capital – in the UK the institutional investors – and those who demand it – industrial companies. Stock market capitalization of a company is not only set by the (normally) small proportion of shares traded, which will set one price, but the potential price of the shares once it becomes known that a quoted company is bidding for another one. The prospect of a gap between the valuation of shares set by marginal trading and that likely to be offered if trading in the shares reaches the dimensions set by its complete takeover offers opportunities for investors to make short-term gains. This opportunity is particularly important to the fund manager who is judged by his ability to maintain or increase the immediate returns from his portfolio. A manager may therefore attach a high rate of discount to investments which pay off in the long run but not in the short run.

One has to be careful in linking up this argument to the complaint of industrialists and others that the City is to blame for their inability to contemplate investments with long lead times and research and development expenditures with delayed pay-off periods. Instituted investors appear to be interested not only in capital values but also in the prospect of high dividends. Companies that seek to finance long-term investment out of earnings will only pay out a small proportion of their earnings as dividends and this will be reflected in lower Price/Earnings ratios and lower valuation ratios as compared with similar companies that distribute a larger proportion of earnings. Undervaluation of a company's shares may make it more vulnerable to takeover, so that companies which perceive that they are under pressure to pay out higher dividends to avoid this threat have to forego long-term investment. However, if that is so, one is bound to ask the question why such companies, if forced to raise their proportion of earnings paid out in dividends, do not then find it easier to raise new money.

If the 'short-termism' thesis were robust, it would be expected that the behaviour of institutional investors, whose decisions are a major influence on the stock market, would conform to a pattern in which short term factors would dominate their attitudes to corporate takeovers. That being so, the Inquiry commissioned Professor and Mrs. Morgan to undertake a survey of attitudes of investment managers of merchant banks, insurance companies, pension funds, investment trusts and unit trusts to takeovers. A questionnaire was sent to 189 large institutions and the response rate of 44 per cent can be regarded as very satisfactory. Small institutions were not approached because of sampling difficulties. Of the 80 respondents who disclosed the size of their total funds, 68 per cent held UK equities of £1bn. or over and 14 per cent had between £0.5bn. and £1bn.

The results of the survey are recorded in detail by Professor and Mrs. Morgan (HOPs 24 and 25) and make a major contribution to our knowledge of institutional attitudes to takeovers. It is sufficient for this analysis to record only those of their findings which throw light on the problem of 'short-termism'.

The first point to be made is that in large financial institutions the decision to accept or reject a bid is, more often than not, made by a professional investment manager on his own authority. It is perhaps not surprising that, in the case of takeovers, the investment managers tend to rely on 'in-house research' rather than on brokers' advice, as with ordinary investment decisions. At the same time, there is a wide dispersion in the number of qualified staff engaged on in-house research. As might be expected, managers of funds over £1bn. tended to be supported by a staff, of, say, 20 or more, but over 30 per cent of all respondents reported 10 or fewer qualified staff, including nearly 20 per cent of those with funds of more than £1bn.

The second point relates to the sources of information considered by investment managers. Managers' perception of the 'offer' and 'defence' documents in contested takeovers displayed considerable scepticism. The rating of these documents was backed by written comments by the respondents and it is interesting, though not surprising, that investment managers saw through attempts to provide financial and other information which was selective and therefore misleading. One of the most forceful comments was that: "it seems quite amazing that the company being bid for miraculously produces a profit in excess of all profit forecasts. Also it is quite astounding how hidden assets in terms of property etc., are suddenly truly valued." (See HOP 24, p.26.)

However, even if it appears that investigation of takeovers by investment managers probed deeply into information provided by predators and targets, and looked more widely than their documentary evidence, the crucial question is whether or not this information led them to take decisions which concentrated on the immediate value of the bid or towards long-term prospects. The third and crucial point is that managers claimed that long-term prospects of both the bidder and target were more important than the immediate value of the bid. Table 4.2 extracted from the survey is of particular interest:

Table 4.2   IMPORTANCE OF FACTORS IN BID DECISIONS

	Number of Respondents				
	Very	Moderate	Little	None	No Response
Long-term prospects of bidder	59	16	3	2	5
Long term prospects of target	74	9	0	0	2
Immediate value of bid	57	22	4	0	2
Gearing of bidder	37	34	5	1	8
Nationality of bidder	1	13	37	30	4
Regional effects	0	11	34	37	3
Effects of employment	1	16	38	26	4
Other	9	3	0	5	68

SOURCE   Questionnaire Survey, Morgan (HOP 25, p.27).
NOTE   Figures refer to number of respondents out of a total of 82.

Clearly, the long-term prospects of the target company and of the bidder were given as more important than the immediate value of the bid itself.

Of course, as is realised by the authors of the Survey, the stated views of managers have to be checked against their actual behaviour in the light of their obligations to their clients. They record elsewhere (HOP 24, pp.62–64) that many financial institutions have short holding periods and regard longer-run performance of companies as being of such little consequence to clients that they might lose them if they took the risk of not going for short-term gains. A rather different survey by Cosh, Hughes and Singh (*op.cit.*) covers a much more limited number of institutions though they conducted in-depth interviews. They claim that "investment returns predominated over industrial logic or changes in underlying real variables in decisions on how to respond to mergers and takeover bids" (p.15). They single out the merchant banks as being under particular pressure from clients to give primacy to short-term performance because of the intense competition for clients, whereas self-managed pension funds and unit trusts were more likely to be able to take a long-term view.

It is difficult to come to a precise conclusion about the relationship between takeover activity and decisions by companies to forego long-term investment under pressure from institutions to pay out dividends. There are clearly other influences on investment decisions by companies which could explain difficulties in funding longer term projects than such pressure. It has been pointed out (e.g. Sykes HOP 23, p.19) that uncertainties created by industrial and economic policies pursued by successive UK governments have inhibited long-term investment. Financial commentators frequently argue that the high gearing of German and Japanese companies both makes firms less dependent on the capital market and links them with institutions such as banks who have a greater appreciation of a company's 'true' prospects. What is probably incontestable is that the institutions under pressure to go for short-term gains must have a strong vested interest in taking advantage of takeover initiatives and thereby encourage such initiatives, whether or not they will result in improvements in economic performance through tighter management and better informed decision-taking in industry.

(c) 'Synergy'?

Whether or not a mutual approach is made between companies (as with a friendly merger) or one company approaches another (as with a takeover), the combined companies must be assumed to confer some advantages on those who initiate these moves. Ever mindful of the professional kudos derived from inventing flashy terminology, some economists refer to this kind of action as illustrating the principle of 'super-additivity' where if the value of one company is x and the company with which it is to be merged or which is taken over is y, then a coalition is expected to produce a value, z, where $z > x + y$ — the '2 + 2 = 5' principle!

Economists offer obvious reasons why takeover may improve the economy's performance, provided that competition is not reduced. 'Super-additivity' may be reflected in economies of scale or marketing and/or in economies of scope where wider product ranges are made possible by exploiting complementarities of production (see Reid, HOP 22). These reasons are often given in takeover bids literature with appropriate appealing terms used such as 'synergy' or 'strategic bundling' to convince shareholders that there is a firm pay-off. There is likely to be endless argument as to whether these reasons are sufficient to raise an expectation that most takeovers are designed to improve performance and will in fact do so. Much depends obviously on whether the changes in managerial structure which inevitably follow takeovers will provide for monitoring procedures which are able to ensure that advantage can be taken of the economies of scale and scope.

As Reid (HOP 22, p.3) indicates, the presence of gains as a result of merger presupposes that the management structure is able to avoid increases in costs in attempts to maintain the incentives to work and to innovate. New 'managerial' theories of the firm have tended to discount 'synergic' gains because of observed monitoring difficulties in the restructured companies. As already observed (see section V above) the targeting of bids may itself be a function of managerial ambitions which conflict with shareholder interests.

It is, of course, possible to argue, as is frequently done, that even the threat of takeover is sufficient to produce some of the effects which might result from a successful bid, so that comparisons between the performance of merged and non-merged companies within an economy must allow for this. However, as Jonathan Charkham has argued, while the fear of contested bids may direct attention towards good financial management, it is doubtful if it encourages risk taking (Charkham (1990)). Whatever the logical consistency of the 'synergy' thesis, it neither offers an explanation of the motives for takeover nor can it be traced in the overall performance of the economy.

VIII   Conclusions on Takeovers and Economic Performance

Several broad conclusions have emerged from this survey of the link between takeovers and economic performance.

i)   The 'efficient market hypothesis', while useful as a starting point for the analysis of the market for corporate control, is based on strong assumptions which are not reflected in the British capital market. In particular, it underestimates the 'agency problem', whereby shareholders have to incur considerable costs in monitoring the activities of institutions who invest on their behalf and of managers who run the companies in which they hold shares or in which shares are held for them.

ii)   Assessment of company performance before and after takeover provide no concrete evidence that takeovers are predominantly 'successful' whatever measure of 'success' (managerial perceptions, profitability, rates of return on capital, shareholder wealth) is used.

iii) There is no evidence to suggest that takeovers have a positive effect on overall economic performance, as measured by rates of investment and growth in GDP. On the contrary, cogent arguments can be advanced suggesting that takeovers may encourage companies to forego long-term investment projects and reflect managerial decisions which improve managerial incomes without a concomitant improvement in managerial performance.

5 Effects of Takeovers on Regional and Local Communities

I Introduction

The subject of this Chapter is a matter of continuous concern and has been frequently investigated particularly in Scotland. Though it is questionable whether this Inquiry can add much to the analysis of regional effects of takeovers, the concentration of interest on the Rowntree/Nestlé takeover makes it necessary to offer an overview of the conclusions reached, particularly those which have a bearing on government (including EEC) policies. The Inquiry's own study of the Rowntree/Nestlé case (see HOP 29) does, however, raise some fresh questions about the methods used in analysing the effects of corporate takeovers.

This Chapter considers the following matters:

i)   data on the net change in regional control of companies as a result of takeover, with particular reference to Scotland;

ii) the methodological problems encountered in identifying and measuring the regional impact of takeovers;

iii) a broad assessment of the effects of takeovers which are of particular public concern.

II Takeovers and Regional Control of Companies

The concentration of interest on the change in the regional pattern of control of companies reflects the generally-held view that this change can be traced through into major changes in regional and local economic and social effects.

The indicator of the pattern of change which is normally used is the net change in company control so that account is taken of 'cross-border' acquisitions. Obviously, inter-regional changes in company control exclude net acquisitions by foreign companies, but reference to international cross-border control is made elsewhere (see HOP 29).

The inquiry commissioned Drs. Ashcroft and Love (A/L) of Strathclyde University to update their already extensive investigations into the regional impact of takeovers. Figures 5.1 and 5.2 are reproduced from HOP 17, p.4:

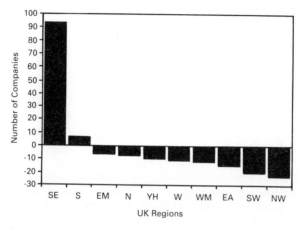

Figure 5.1   Cumulative Transfers of Net Control UK Regions: 1968 to 1985

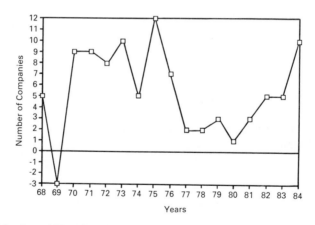

Figure 5.2   Annual Transfer of Net Control to South East from Region 1968 to 1985

Figure 5.1 shows the cumulative net change in regional control by takeover for the larger UK companies over the period 1968–85 for each standard region: SE = South East, S = Scotland, EM = East Midlands, N = North, YH = Yorkshire and Humberside, W = Wales, WM = West Midlands, EA = East Anglia, SW = South West and NW = North West. Figure 5.2 displays the annual net transfer of control to the SE from the other British regions. The balance clearly shifts towards the SE and, as

A/L emphasise, the imbalance may indeed be under-estimated by these calculations. This is because firms in the Rest of Britain who take over firms in the South East may use takeover in order to effect a transfer of their headquarters to London.

This trend is corroborated by the survey of unquoted companies carried out by Graham Bannock and Partners and reported in Bannock (HOP 15, p.15), commissioned for the Inquiry. The percentage of unquoted companies intending to make one or more acquisitions during 1990 was much higher in Greater London than in the North East and Scotland.

While the change in the pattern of control helps to put the regional dimension of takeover into perspective, the importance of control can only be gauged by the relative size of the acquired companies, as measured for example, by turnover, value added, profit, employment and other relevant indicators. There is very little reliable information about the 'net' position of regions. Some guesses have been made for Scotland, a region for which documentation on takeovers is extensive. It will be noted that Scotland was a 'net acquirer' of companies during 1968–85, but, according to Richardson and Turok (1990), "Scottish companies do not appear to have made takeover bids comparable in size to the largest inward acquisitions" (p.10). No evidence has been submitted to us which suggests that the relative size of companies acquired by British regions other than the SE compensates for the imbalance in the number of takeovers.

The fact of growing concentration of control in the South East offers sufficient evidence for concern about the effect of this concentration on regional and local economies. The Inquiry might simply proceed now to examine whether this concentration of control results in major changes in regional and local economic structure. It is nevertheless of interest to examine some of the characteristics of the acquired firms where data are available. Richardson and Turok (*op.cit.*) conducted a survey of 32 firms in Scotland most of which were taken over during the boom year 1986/87. We summarize their findings as follows:

i)   The bulk of firms were taken over by acquirers with HQs in Britain, as many as 17 (53%) being taken over by SE England-based companies.

ii) There was a considerable variation in size distribution as measured by employment, turnover or assets.

iii) In all but two cases, the bidding firms were larger than the firms acquired.

iv) Two-thirds of the firms were private limited companies, but the remaining third, which were PLCs, were generally much larger, as one would expect.

v)   Three-quarters of the firms were in the manufacturing sector, with a concentration in scientific instruments and electronics.

vi) Just over half the takeovers were initiated by the acquirers. There were only four 'hostile' bids but these were all large PLCs with turnover in excess of £20m.

vii) The main reason given by firms for 'seeking or accepting takeover' was improvement in access to finance. Bidders gave as their main reason the desire to expand their market share.

III Modelling the Regional Impact of Takeovers

Clearly, a change in the control over a company implies possible changes in the objectives which the company is expected to achieve, with consequential changes in its organisation and working methods and in the pattern of its links, through buying and selling, with customers and suppliers. Not unnaturally, regional concern is less with the overall performance of the acquiring company, as measured by rates of profit and market share, and more with the effects of the structural changes introduced in the acquired company which are reflected in employment patterns. These concerns cover not only the direct employment effects, including the redistribution of managerial functions as well as changes in the labour force, but also the indirect or 'linkage' effects produced by the change in the pattern of purchases of raw material inputs and of services. The contrast with appraisal based purely on overall economic performance is even greater when account is taken of the less tangible effects such as how a 'dependency' image affects local business morale and sharpens the interest of the young and enterprising in trying their luck elsewhere. In short, there is a groundswell of strong feeling in regional communities which fosters intense suspicion of 'selling out to foreigners', even those who live within the same borders. Even with a different basis of appraisal, there are similar methodological problems in testing the commonly made statements about the regional effects of takeovers.

The first of these problems concerns the identification of a 'loss of regional control' of a company, for it is commonly supposed that an external takeover must result in a different outcome than that which would occur if the company remained independent. As A/L point out (HOP 17, p.12), what constitute 'regional location' and 'regional control' are not so easy to determine. The spectrum of regional concentration may range from an independent company with only one plant to a company with locations in several regions and even with several plants abroad. An acquisition or takeover of one part of the company outside the region may affect the activities within the region. It seems sensible, as A/L do, to define 'control' in terms of the location of the headquarters of the company. This means that the issue of most concern is whether this ultimate control affects operations in a particular region in which the HQ is not located. However, this also implies that if the 'foreign' company is taken over – and this may very well result in changes in the operations conducted in a particular region – this does not count as a loss of regional control. A/L defend their position by arguing that "only a change in location of an existing degree of external control rather than a change in the level or extent of external control *per se* constitutes the kind of change which is relevant to the discussion". This Inquiry goes along with their 'HQ definition' of control, if only on pragmatic grounds.

The second problem is one already encountered in analysing takeovers in general. The regional impact of a takeover by a 'foreign' company cannot be measured simply by looking solely at the performance of a company before and after acquisition. That performance has to be compared with some 'counterfactual' position representing what would otherwise have happened to company performance if takeover had not occurred. Clearly, there is much room for argument about what would constitute an inevitably hypothetical alternative. The approach used by A/L is on all fours with methods described in Chapter 4 section IV above. The hypothetical performance of the company, had takeover not taken place, is based on its performance in relation to its position within its own industry, which entails identifying its performance in relation to the average performance. (For fuller discussion see Ashcroft, Love and Scouler.) This approach is certainly more satisfactory than that implicit in much popular discussion in which it is assumed that the 'counterfactual' is simply no change in the variables of interest, such as employment, incomes, and investment, and there appear to be sufficient statistical data upon which reasonable estimates of the variables can be made.

Getting the definition of 'regional control' right and getting the 'model' right are not the only difficulties. Whichever 'comparator' is used, it must be possible to obtain accurate data of pre- and post-acquisition trends in those variables which are of public concern, such as profitability changes, job losses and the like. Company data supplemented by official statistics will go a long way to help in this respect, but much is made in public discussion of the 'knock-on' effects of changes by acquisition, such as changes in the demand for inputs of raw materials and services from local suppliers, already mentioned. (It should be stressed that the 'counterfactual' position must also be clarified in regard to these changes as well.) Obtaining such information normally requires direct inquiry from individual companies and aggregation of these 'input-output' relations is an expensive operation often requiring heroic assumptions to be made. Regional input-output tables are therefore rare and their lag in preparation and infrequent publication limit their practical use. It may be possible to indicate the direction of the changes produced in input-output patterns, but magnitudes, including 'second round' effects, are difficult to establish. Nor is it simply a question of determining the direction and magnitude of the 'ripples' produced by a change in ownership on companies' operations, but also the length of time taken for these secondary effects to materialise. To illustrate these complications, assume that a Scots company taken over by a SE predator is ordered to shift its purchases of raw materials from Scots suppliers to English suppliers. There may be a short-term fall in incomes and employment in the Scots firms, but it is not necessarily the case that these firms will react purely passively to this situation and in the longer term they may be able to secure other markets. (Such a reaction suggests, however, that if competition is keen, the result may be a reduction in the demand for the products, and therefore a fall in the incomes and employment, in competing non-acquired firms!). The output and employment of the English suppliers may expand, and it is even possible that this expansion may occasion an increase in purchases of its raw materials from Scots firms. Clearly, the magnitude and speed of the chain reaction is highly complicated, but its existence must be recognized.

The Inquiry has sought, wherever possible, to collect and examine empirical evidence on the effect of takeovers but such evidence has distinct limitations in coming to firm conclusions about their regional effects. It has, however, had useful guidance from a number of investigators who have concentrated primarily on what has happened in Scotland, where the external control of its economy has been a burning issue. In the following section, much of the evidence is derived from Scots experience.

IV Effects of Takeovers on the Regional Economy

To be on all fours with 'indicators of success' used in assessing takeover performance, the starting point should be the changes in profitability of companies taken over in regions. There is little evidence to go on. A/L record that in their previous work (see Ashcroft, Love and Scouler (1987) (ALS) on Scotland alone, they analysed acquired companies' profit and sales performance using return on capital employed (ROCE) and return on sales (ROS). They took a period of ten years, comparing the performance of companies five years before and five years after takeover. In the case of both ROCE and ROS, a statistically significant deterioration was found, though sales performance by itself improved markedly. We could hardly expect the authors to fall into their own trap and not make the point that such a comparison ignores the counterfactual situation! When a 'comparator' is introduced which identifies the position of each firm relative to industry performance, then the post-acquisition performance of ROCE is practically unchanged, whereas the negative effect on ROS is still found. The positive effect on sales is also eliminated. These results are not altogether surprising when viewed against the evidence provided in Chapter 4.

The effects of regional takeovers on employment give rise to much concern. Partly for this reason and partly because statistical data on employment are easy to collect, much evidence has been provided on this aspect though it is not always easy to interpret. Before examining this, it is worth pausing to consider, albeit briefly, how takeovers seem likely to affect employment. It is here that the motives for takeover are important. Improving profitability in competitive markets immediately suggests that, unless there is a change in the product mix, productivity improvements are required. In 'tough' markets, notably in manufacturing, this may require labour shedding and even plant closures; and these are the consequences which are naturally feared in regions in which traditional manufacturing industry may be concentrated. However, our previous analysis of managerial motivation (Chapter 4, Section VI) suggests that acquisitions are more likely to be motivated by the desire for growth. Vertical integration in which expertise in new processes can be sought out could be an important factor in cutting costs. (Acquisitions in order to secure R and D skills have been a feature in Scotland.) Horizontal integration is a more direct way of seeking growth objectives by diversification into new lines of business. These factors are mentioned only as a reminder of the highly complex nature of the strategies of bidding companies, and sufficient has been said about them here and elsewhere in the Report to explain the concern expressed in regions about the effects of takeovers not only on the amount but also on the *pattern* of both direct and indirect employment.

As A/L explain, much of the earlier work on the regional effects of takeovers seemed to suggest that the aggregate direct employment effects were substantially negative (see A/L HOP 17, p.21). However, such studies either ignored or had difficulty in taking account of the methodological snags in defining a regional takeover and in identifying a suitable counterfactual position. A/L record that their own extensive work on employment effects in Scotland found "no significant effect of acquisition....although there was a tendency for public companies to fare significantly worse than private companies following takeover. Given that peripheral regional economies tend to have relatively few public companies and that these tend to be the largest employers, this may be a finding of some significance. Overall, evidence to date appears to indicate that external acquisition is unlikely to be beneficial to the employment of acquired companies in the short to medium term, although there is equally little systematic evidence of detriment". The later study by Richardson and Turok (1990) already mentioned and covering the period 1982–89 adopts an in-depth approach involving the study of 29 firms and, instead of using a comparator, tries to identify in each case the changes that occurred 'as a direct result of takeovers'. These results had to be derived from interviews and, as the authors admit, even those closely affected by takeovers have difficulty in identifying the 'attributable effects' (See R/T, section 4.) They record that their results are 'slightly more negative' than A/L, but more interest attaches to the incidence of job losses.

i) Losses were concentrated in acquired firms in traditional industries such as textiles, engineering and metal manufacturing, whereas employment in acquired firms in printing, electronics and services expanded.

ii) There was no obvious link between hostile bids and job losses.

iii) There appeared to be no connexion between firm size and post-acquisition performance.

A matter of equal concern in regions is the effect of corporate takeovers on the composition of factor inputs. Decisions taken outside the region may result in a change in the product mix with consequential changes in the proportions of men and women employed, in the mix of skills required and shifts in demand between whole-time and part-time labour. Whether or not there is a change in the product mix, long-term planning decisions will be taken outside the region – with an obvious bias towards S.E. England. This may entail the local reduction in the staff of the acquired company concerned with such functions as marketing, research and development, for such staff will now be concentrated at headquarters.

Taking the labour force first, there appears to be general agreement that the effects on the composition of the labour force are marginal. The position is summed up by R/T in their study of 29 firms, as follows. "In fact, there is very little change in the proportions of male to female workers; blue collar to white collar workers; and management to the remaining workforce. The only significant change was that four firms reported an increase in the ratio of skilled to unskilled workers". A/L/S and R/T also agree that fears of "technological asset-stripping" resulting in reduction in research staff engaged on R and D in indigenous firms were unfounded. The most significant change related to the duties of management staff. Whereas the number of management staff might not change greatly, their function tended to move away from entrepreneurial decision-making which would have a major effect on the company's operations towards routine managerial tasks such as monitoring the output of the work force. For example, half of the firms in the A/L/S study sample experienced reductions in staff engaged in 'key' functions including purchasing and marketing. In the R/T sample, there was a significant decrease detected in the number of management staff and in seven cases new staff from the acquiring firms replaced existing managers.

Earlier it was pointed out that the 'chain reaction' set up by any change in the amount and composition of raw material and services inputs was difficult to express in quantitative form. What little evidence there is (cf.R/T p.36) suggests that the effect on local material inputs was, if anything, slight. However, along with the direct impact resulting in a fall in demand for top management staff, there appears to have been a quite significant reduction in service inputs, notably in banking and insurance services. This clearly reflected the transfer of decisions regarding finance to the centre. It is a trend which is regarded as particularly disturbing in Scotland where a determined attempt has been made, through Scottish Financial Enterprise, to retain and develop financial expertise in everything from banking to pension fund management (See Scottish Financial Enterprise, 1989).

V Regional Effects of Takeovers and National Policies

It seems to be generally agreed amongst specialists that the evidence concerning regional takeovers in Scotland is a fair guide to the general situation caused by headquarters concentration in S.E. England. That being the case, the main concern is the negative effect of regional takeovers on the retention in the regions of entrepreneurial and managerial skills. This concern is shared by The Scottish Office and is given expression in their Memorandum of Evidence to the Inquiry (See HOP 27, p.4). The Office raises this point in relation to their recent reaction to the attempt by Elders IXL to take over Scottish and Newcastle Breweries: "We argued .... that there was likely to be a loss of some or all of Scottish and Newcastle's headquarters functions and the purchase of associated services from Edinburgh. This would make it more difficult to attract and retain high calibre people in the Scottish economy and contribute to a longer term process of erosion of indigenous entrepreneurial capacity".

From a regional perspective, the reduction in the quality of entrepreneurship and management skills must be regarded as being to the detriment of both its economic and social life. Business and professional leadership has spillover effects on the maintenance of interest in and concern for the arts and culture generally not only in the giving of advice but in active participation in the governance of a whole variety of non-profit-making and charitable institutions designed to improve the quality of life. A value judgment clearly underpins the view that regional dispersal of professional talent is wholly desirable but it is one which is widely held. "Maintaining and promoting the balanced distribution of industry and employment" is a component of the definition of 'the public interest' as laid down in the 1973 Fair Trading Act and has to be considered by the Monopolies and Mergers Commission when takeover bids are referred to it. Where disagreement is bound to arise is in specifying the trade-off between inter-regional equity and the objective of maximising the growth performance of the economy, implying the fostering of competition and the removal of obstructions to the creation of a market for corporate control.

This Report takes no position on the evaluation of the inter-regional equity and overall growth performance objectives, but offers two points for consideration which need to be borne in mind by anyone making such an evaluation and with takeovers in mind.

It has been put to the Inquiry that decentralised decision-making in industry is not in competition with the object of maintaining the growth performance of the economy as a whole, but complementary to it. Accordingly, any factor, such as takeover, which fosters concentration of industrial and economic power in the SE, will act as a deterrent to national economic progress. It is presumably argued that any economies of scale resulting from concentration of financial and managerial services in the SE will be offset by 'diseconomies' resulting from increases in congestion and possibly pollution from population concentration. The point is worth making although it is difficult to produce incontrovertible evidence in favour of either position on economies of scale.

A final point is that our Inquiry has not established that regional takeovers are a major cause of regional disparities of incomes and employment. If that were the case, one would expect to find a close correlation between the growth in the annual transfer of net control (See Table 5.2) and regional disparities in income and employment. No such association can be traced in the available data. In any case, when investigating national economic performance, one may be sure that just as there are many influences on firms' investment decisions other than the incidence of takeovers, so there are many other causes of regional disparities. It is certainly not the purpose of this Inquiry to digress into this more fundamental question.

PART III: POLICY

6 Present Government Policy and Takeovers

I Introduction

There is an enormous contemporary literature reviewing government policies covering mergers and takeovers. The David Hume Institute has paid particular attention to the issues, notably in two papers by Professor Morgan (See HOP 5 and Hume Paper 7). The DTI Blue Paper on Mergers Policy (1988) discusses in some detail the policies and procedures of merger control and paved the way for some changes in mergers policy which reflected the growing concern about the acceleration of takeover activities. Latterly, the Trade and Industry Committee has received a mass of evidence from both governmental and non-governmental sources. (See House of Commons, 1991.)

The problem of reviewing merger policies without recourse to a major digression into industrial policy *in toto* has been facilitated by the willingness of the DTI, the Scottish Office, and the Office of Fair Trading to highlight those elements of policy that they regard as important in Memoranda of Evidence submitted to this Inquiry. The Inquiry is grateful to all of them for their assistance. Additionally, we received much appreciated help from Sir Leon Brittan and his staff at the EC Commission in the preparation of the report on EC policy.

During the period of operation of this Inquiry the EC Merger Control Regulation agreed by the Internal Market Council of the EC in December 1989 came into effect. This Regulation has given the EC a major role to play in the implementation of merger policy. The Inquiry commissioned a separate report by Robert Pringle (HOP 29) which examines the European dimension to merger and takeover policy in detail. The aims of EC policy towards mergers are closely allied to those of the British Government. As DTI state in their evidence (HOP 18, pp.37–39), the powers afforded to EC "mirror the UK's own policy". There is still pronounced disagreement within EC about the extent to which the rules governing takeover should be harmonised and it is not sensible for us to predict the outcome of the EC Commission's efforts to develop the necessary company law which would conform to harmonisation objectives. Nevertheless we draw attention to some of the issues to which this new European policy dimension gives rise. (See Section V below.)

II Aims of Present Government Policy

In stark contrast with the previous Conservative Government and with the succeeding Labour Government of 1974–79, the present Government's industrial strategy is built round the promotion of competition, and this Report has already quoted *in extenso* the DTI's expression of this view. Accordingly, "the market should be allowed to decide whether a merger should go ahead, since the free commercial decisions of private decision makers tend to result in the most desirable outcomes for the economy as a whole" (HOP 18, p.28. See also *Blue Paper on Merger Policy*, Chapter 2.) The DTI confirmed its view in evidence to the House of Commons Trade and Industry Committee. (See H.C. 226–i p.5.)

The principal reason for intervening in cases where mergers are contemplated lies in the possibility that in the process of merging, competition itself becomes more restricted. This is described as the 'primary grounds for reference' (HOP 18, p.33). Other grounds for reference are considered, particularly as our terms of reference extend to wider issues than economic performance, but are largely dismissed. The reasons given in each case are of considerable interest.

First, take regional or local effects. The DTI evidence recognises mergers may have particular and immediate effects on local employment prospects and have social and cultural effects associated with the movement of companies' headquarters away from the locality or region. The DTI consideration of regional concerns follows very much our previous line of argument. Rationalisation by merger is only one technique used by businesses to maintain their profitability in a competitive world. If mergers at regional level were to be disallowed this would not "impose any obligation on the incumbent management to preserve the status quo" (HOP 18, p.33). A dig is made at our Inquiry Synopsis which raised the issue of "fear that multinationals of other countries are more ruthless in their hiring and firing policies and take less account of their actions on local incomes and employment". The DTI evidence counters: "(t)he Government believes that to seize on the potential adverse effects of a merger .... as a reason for preventing it from proceeding would drastically reduce the economy's flexibility and adaptibility to change, which is an essential precondition for success in a world of rapidly changing markets" (HOP 18, p.34). The Inquiry was surely right to raise this issue and to discuss it in detail (see Chapter 5) while coming to much the same conclusion as the DTI that "regional issues are best addressed by other regional policies, not by mergers policy" (HOP 18, p.34).

The second possible qualification to the general thrust of policy concerns direct inward investment which takes place through the acquisition of existing companies. The criterion of preserving and improving competition points towards welcoming such investment, provided that a two-way flow is maintained. Because UK companies engage in acquisition of overseas companies on a considerable scale, the Government is sensitive to the issue of the degree to which reciprocal freedom of acquisition exists, having regard to complaints about higher barriers to entry, particularly those raised by EC partners. Again, the Government argue that the way forward is not to raise barriers against inward investment but to negotiate with trading partners to lower barriers in conformity with the EC Commission's efforts to remove them as part of the 'single market' objective.

The attention paid to the regional issue and to the conditions governing cross-border bidding is understandable but it is difficult fully to understand why the DTI evidence picks out highly leveraged bids as the third item in its list of possible additional reasons for intervention. There are several other aspects of the acquisition process which might command equal attention. This may represent a reaction to the adverse publicity given to hostile bids in which bond financing has resulted in a high interest debt burden as well as a short period of debt repayment. The result, more marked in the USA than in the UK, has frequently been widespread asset sales and pressures on short-term profits, which suggests that highly leveraged bids have adverse effects on the growth in capital investment. On a large scale this could be regarded as against the public interest as it could affect long-run economic performance of the economy. Again, the DTI dismisses a case for specific intervention. It does so on the grounds (see HOP 18, pp.34–35) that shareholders will have received adequate warning of the dangers of high leverage from recent experiences, as for example in the recent collapse of Drexel, and 'sensible judgments' by the market leading to rejection of highly leveraged bids do take place. At the same time, there could be instances where the increase in leverage might result in assets being put to more efficient use than would be the case were the target company left untouched by takeover. If there are grounds for questioning a takeover of this sort, it will generally be because high leverage is one of a number of features of the bid which "pose dangers to the public interest".

The fourth item in the list of supplementary aims concerns the effect of takeovers on R and D spending. The case rests on the presumption that R and D spending in the target company will be cut by an acquirer in order to increase short-term profitability, thereby neglecting the long-term future of the company. This argument is given short shrift by the DTI who argue that "it is equally possible that the existing management will make bad decisions, whether on R and D or on other investments"... and .... "it is not normally for Government to adjudicate between the R and D plans of rival managements: that is a matter for the shareholders."

The final item was added by the Secretary of State, Mr. Peter Lilley, in July 1990. Particular attention will now be directed towards mergers which might increase the degree of state control. This could happen through acquisitions by public corporations, U.K. and foreign, which are not subject to the competitive forces operating in the private sector. 'Back door' nationalization could not only reduce the scope of competitive forces but would extend the influence of managements not required to conform to commercial criteria.

Before considering methods of merger control, it must be emphasised that it is an important facet of mergers policy that the Government does not take a conspiratorial view of mergers as a source of anti-competitive activity. On the contrary, as the Office of Fair Trading Memorandum of Evidence (HOP 18, pp.17) points out, the primary objectives of mergers policy are two-fold. The first objective is to identify and prevent mergers that do reduce competition but also "to allow mergers to go ahead *with the least possible delay or impediment*" (italics ours).

III Policy Instruments

Given that the main concern of Government about mergers lies in the possible restriction of competition, its first task is to *identify* mergers which appear to be anti-competitive.

The principal merger control legislation is to be found in the Fair Trading Act 1973. It specifies the role of the governmental bodies concerned with the process of investigation of mergers. As stated by the Director General of Fair Trading (HOP 18, p.18) "The Director General *advises*, the Secretary of State *decides*, the MMC *investigates*". It lays down two tests for prima facie investigation of a merger. The first is a market share test of 25 per cent of any market in the UK, a reduction from the 33 per cent test which operated until 1973. The second test is an 'assets criterion' which, as stated in money terms, is subject to adjustment to allow for inflation. At present this figure is set at £30m, though no adjustment has taken place since 1984. It is important to note that the law makes no distinction between contested and uncontested mergers. 'Hostile' bids will only come within the purview of the DG. of Fair Trading if they meet one or other of the two tests.

In recent years, mergers identified by these tests as qualifying under the Fair Trading Act have represented somewhere between a fifth and a third of all takeovers by industrial and commercial companies. The definition of mergers and acquisitions follows that of the Central Statistical Office's Business Bulletin which collects information on mergers mainly from press reports. As pointed out earlier, this definition excludes large numbers of smaller acquisitions which remain unrecorded.

The fact that a merger or acquisition is identified by the two criteria does not mean that it is automatically referred to the Secretary of State for Trade and Industry (S of S) as having "too much" market power. There is an intermediate weeding out stage which brings into play the OFT's task of analysing the foreseeable effect on competition. This can be quite an elaborate process, the main features of which embody the usual list of tests invented by economists, notably the market share, the availability of substitutes, the structure of the market for inputs, and the 'contestability' of the market by possible new entrants including overseas actual or potential competitors. (The OFT offers a more detailed list in HOP 18, pp.22–24.) The OFT report that over the last 10 years or so they have examined anything from between 150 and 350 qualifying mergers per year but that the maximum actually recommended for further investigation has not exceeded 14 in any one year. This represents only about 1 per cent of all mergers, as defined by the CSO.

In applying the criteria, it should be noted that there will be occasions when OFT will pick out mergers or acquisitions which may have anti-competitive effects at the local or regional level, an example being bus services. If the 'market' were defined in national terms, then a bus company, for example, might be providing only a very small part of the total output of bus services, but this would not prevent it having a marked effect on price and the quality of service in a specific area. The Fair Trading Act recognises that local monopoly power should be considered provided it operates in a 'substantial part of the UK'. The OFT in their evidence emphasise that "these are examples of cases where a competition objection was perceived in a local market. It is not current policy to refer solely because a merger might have some detrimental economic effects in a region, e.g. the move of operations from one part of the country to another" (HOP 18, p.25).

If the OFT recommends that a merger be referred to the MMC for investigation it is not automatically passed on by the DTI. It is for the Secretary of State to decide whether it is in the public interest to have the MMC investigate the merger. In the last analysis this is a political decision. The DTI's own staff appraise the technical arguments of the OFT and review the case in terms of the requirements of the Companies Act 1989 which gives the power to the Secretary of State to accept undertakings by companies engaged in merger activity without requiring him to refer the case to the MMC. In doing so, the Secretary of State is advised by the OFT, who can recommend that a company be given the opportunity to divest itself of part of a merged enterprise. This provision is clearly designed to speed up the decision making process, for then the merger, modified by agreement of this kind, can go ahead. Once the Secretary of State decides to refer a merger to the MMC, a bid lapses automatically (see discussion of Takeover Code below), and the firm is at the mercy of the MMC's timetable. There is also an automatic prohibition of share acquisitions during an MMC investigation.

Why it should be necessary for the Secretary of State to require further investigation after a recommendation by the OFT is a matter requiring some explanation. The OFT's remit is wide, and covers all aspects of the restriction of competition of which mergers are only one possible source. The MMC is concerned more specifically with monopolies and mergers. It is not there to establish the fact of loss of potential competition as a result of a merger, but with the consequences. Indeed, while the primary aim of policy may be promotion of competition, the 'public interest' to which the MMC has to address itself is considered in much wider terms. Alongside the promotion of competition, the MMC has to consider the effects of mergers on the distribution of industry and employment within the UK; there is even a blanket clause in the Fair Trading Act which enjoins the MMC to take account of "all matters which appear to them in the particular circumstances to be relevant" (S.84 (1)). It is under this clause that arguments may be brought to it showing that the economies of scale flowing from a particular merger will outweigh any possible restriction on competition.

If the MMC finds that a merger operates against the public interest, the Secretary of State is empowered to issue an order prohibiting it. In most cases, mergers are usually abandoned before such a formal procedure is invoked. The Secretary of State is not obliged to prohibit a merger if the MMC so recommends, but only occasionally will he allow it to proceed. What is important is that the Secretary of State has no power to stop a merger unless the MMC reports that its operations are detrimental to the public interest. Of the 83 references made between 1965 and 1985, 38 were cleared by the MMC, 23 were found to be against the public interest, and 22 were abandoned before the hearings ended.

So far our Report has concentrated on the powers conferred on the DTI, OFT and MMC by fair trading legislation. An important facet of control of takeovers is associated with the process by which a takeover is engineered, a subject which has aroused considerable critical comment (cf. Chapter IV above). The DTI has a general interest in and control of this process through the operation of legislation covering companies. More specifically, following the review of mergers policy in 1988, two important provisions were included in the Companies Act 1989 whereby (i) companies must disclose that they have knowingly built up a holding of more than 3 per cent in the equity of another company; and (ii) misleading information given to the OFT of MMC would be treated as a criminal offence. However, the regulation of the takeover process has been left to voluntary arrangements – in keeping with the government's attitude to the regulation of the financial sector following the 'big bang' in 1986. This requires us to outline the activities of the Takeover Panel which, although not a statutory body, would have had to be invented by government, if it did not exist.

Consideration of the role of the UK Panel on Takeovers and Mergers formed an integral part of the Inquiry and an appraisal of it was undertaken by Mr. W.A.P. Manser and published separately as HOP 21. Here we only outline the main principles and rules of this important body, though we shall refer to specific aspects of its work in later discussion. (See the summary of HOP 21 below, and the research report itself for more detailed discussion). The Panel goes back to 1968, but its present form follows from the passing of the Financial Services Act, 1986, which recognized it as a self-regulatory organisation with membership derived from representative bodies of major institutional investors (e.g. Association of Investment Trust Companies, the Unit Trust Association, together with professional accounting bodies, the Stock Exchange and the Confederation of British Industry).

The most important single objective of the Panel is to protect the interests of shareholders, recognizing that a takeover is essentially a Stock Exchange transaction. The general principles of operation, therefore, are that in a takeover the shareholder is entitled to full, accurate and public information and a fair method of share acquisition.

The rules implementing the first principle are quite elaborate but the essential point is that the shareholders of the 'offeree' company must be immediately informed of any offer, that the amount of information accompanying this announcement must be maximised and include such matters as the identity of the 'offeror', the number of shares held by the offeror and the conditions attached to the offer. Such information must meet prescribed standards and the offeree must seek the views of an independent financial expert which must be circulated to all shareholders.

Likewise the rules following from the second principle are elaborate and complicated. In essence, they are designed to give shareholders time to size up whether or not a bid is likely to be made and the merits of the bid itself. In addition, equality of treatment in the 'consideration' attached to payment made for shares acquired by the offeror is expected, whether it is cash, offeror company shares, loan notes or whatever. Of particular importance are, first, the fixing of the terms of an offer to purchase shares by the offeror. Thus any party who passes a threshold of 30 per cent holding of the shares of the offeree must make an immediate cash offer for all shares. Second, this obligatory cash offer must remain open throughout the period of the offer and is extended until the offeror is able to declare that his bid has been successful, i.e. he holds (or has accepted shares offered to him) which equal at least 50 per cent of the voting rights plus one share. These are only examples which give the flavour of very complicated and extensive rules.

Although the Code is not legally enforceable, the Panel has three important weapons which offer sanctions against non-compliance. The first is the threat of public censure and therefore adverse publicity. The second is that if a takeover bid goes 'sour' and parties feel aggrieved and have recourse to law, the courts, in any judicial review, will normally rely on the Panel's findings and may only be willing to offer such a review when such findings are completed. The third is that the Panel's members commit themselves to withdraw their services from any offender against the rules. For example, the withdrawal of the services of the Stock Exchange will effectively terminate a bid. If any of the new self-regulatory bodies represented on the panel declares an offender as not a 'fit and proper person' to carry on a business, such a ban can be enforced by prosecution under the criminal law.

There are therefore three courses open to offerors in a takeover bid. The first is to co-operate with the Panel, who encourage all parties to seek advice in following the Code and monitor the course of all takeover bids. The second is to reject the ruling of the Panel, which any offeror or offeree can do in principle. Manser reports (HOP 21, p.13) that there is only one known case where this has happened, and, in the end, the 'offender' acceded to the Panel's requirements. The third is to conceal breaches of the rules. A notorious example where this happened was in the famous Guinness bid for Distillers in which the offeror had to pay £85m in compensation to Distillers' shareholders.

IV   Conclusions on Existing National Policies

This whistle-stop tour through present policies towards takeovers can only draw attention to the broad outlines of the policy terrain. More detailed matters will be pursued in reviewing criticism made of their practical effect (See Chapter 7). The reader can review the terrain more closely in the research reports and submitted evidence to which reference has already been made. Nevertheless, some general conclusions can be drawn.

As repeatedly stressed, the Government sees the process of merger and, more particularly, takeovers as an integral part of the working of the competitive market. There is nothing inherently wrong in takeovers, and, so it is believed, a good deal that is right if the result is a more efficient use of capital assets. Therefore, as the DTI state (HOP 18, p.21) "(t)he presumption underlying policy is that, in general, the decision on whether a merger should be allowed to proceed is best left to those whose money is at stake. It is not the role of the Government or statutory agencies to second-guess commercial judgements". (This is a direct quotation from the Blue Paper on Mergers Policy without the addition of the interesting sentence: "Indeed, they are more likely than private decision-makers to make mistaken commercial judgements"!)

Two propositions follow from this general position. The first is that if a takeover is made the subject of investigation, then each case must be considered on its merits. No view is taken on the process of takeover as such, but each must be judged in terms of its effects, notably in respect of its influence on the competitive process. This position explains the Government's reluctance to place the onus of proof as to whether a merger or takeover is in the public interest on the parties involved. The most the Government expects is that an early warning system must be in operation about takeover activity. Even the prenotification of a merger to the OFT, while encouraged, is voluntary.

The second is that pressure must be put on the referral and investigatory process in order to minimize the time taken to come to a decision. As the OFT evidence points out (HOP 18, p.27), MMC investigations of referred mergers are expected to be completed in about three months, whereas six months used to be par for the course.

In summing up the attitude of the present Government we can do no better than to quote the final words of the DTI evidence to the Inquiry (HOP 18, p.39):

> This Memorandum ...... has taken the opportunity to re-state the rationale behind the Government's general approach to this question, which is that competition must be paramount. When regulatory systems attempt to move away from this core concept, it is the consumers – and ultimately the industries themselves, together with the people who work in them – who suffer.

V The Impact of the EC

In the course of the Inquiry's deliberations, the EC adopted a regulation on Mergers in December 1989 which came into force in September of last year. The regulation was the natural concomitant to the move towards a European single market, and no doubt its timing reflected not only the timetable but also the merger boom in EC countries which was partly stimulated by the expected pressure of international competition once the single market is in being. (It is beyond the scope of this Inquiry to review the EC situation in detail, but see the commissioned study by Pringle, (HOP 29) for further information and discussion.) The concern of this Inquiry is how far an EC policy towards mergers is likely to modify the impact of national mechanisms for takeover control.

There are two vital stages in the process of takeover with which governments are closely concerned. The first is to decide whether a takeover is to be allowed to proceed. The second is to approve the rules which govern the transfer of corporate control, having regard to the interests of those who are affected by takeover, particularly shareholders. As this Report has observed in several places, this latter stage operates in very different ways in different countries, depending on the thrust of their company legislation. The question of harmonizing takeover rules has only been touched on by EC, so that a fundamental policy question has largely been left on one side, despite the fact that barriers to transfer of corporate control may be regarded as contrary to the aims of the single market.

This means that the thrust of EC policy lies in subjecting companies to the 'competition test' when mergers are contemplated. As Sir Leon Brittan, Commissioner in charge of EC competition policy, has put it: "We have no view about whether mergers are good or bad or about whether a giant merger is likely to succeed or fail. That is for companies and their shareholders to decide. My task is to discover which mergers threaten competition. They will be stopped. All others will proceed." (Brittan as quoted by Pringle in HOP 29.)

For the purposes of the argument, our interest must lie in the extent to which the EC regulation might override and conflict with British legislation and self-regulation. The following provisions are relevant.

i) A merger will be subject to notification and examination by the Commission if (a) the aggregate worldwide turnover of all firms involved is more than ECU 5b. (approx. £3.5b); and (b) if the aggregate EC-wide turnover of each of at least two of the firms involved is more than ECU 250m. (approx. £175m). These thresholds are due to be reviewed in 1993, when the Commission is expected to propose to the Council of Ministers a substantial reduction in these thresholds.

ii) A strict time limit of one month is set on the opening of proceedings and of four months to conclude proceedings, if these are initiated.

iii) The sole test as to whether a merger is incompatible with the single market is if it "creates or strengthens a dominant position as a result of which competition would be significantly impeded".

iv) The Commission intends to open a 'one-stop shop' so that a merger cleared by it will not generally be prohibited or subjected to conditions by national merger control authorities.

v) There are two exceptions to (iv) above. Members may interfere in a merger to protect 'other legitimate interests' not so far subject to EC rules. However, such measures cannot be taken before the Commission has decided whether they are compatible with Community Law. The second exception allowed by the regulation concerns the application of national competition law to cases where a merger could take up a dominant position in a 'distinct market' within national boundaries. This exception was included to satisfy the German authorities who were reluctant to allow the EC commission to override its own strict application of competition law.

It has already been indicated that the general thrust of EC policy towards mergers has been approved by the British Government, at least in respect of its strong emphasis on the competition criterion. DTI efforts are now being concentrated on the removal of barriers in the single market which unreasonably restrict transfer of corporate control, such as differential voting rights designed to protect existing managements and the ability of management to 'frustrate' shareholders' rights by such devices as 'poison pills'. (For detail, see DTI Memorandum in H.C. 226–i, 1991.)

At the time of writing, of the 16 mergers so far notified to the Commission (to end-January 1991), none has produced sources of conflict between it and national governments, at least in respect of the jurisdiction of the EC and national merger control authorities. In the initial stages of implementation, national governments are likely to be more concerned with whether the regulation is interpreted in a way that ensures consistency of treatment of cases referred to the Commission.

It may not be profitable to speculate on how far harmony will prevail between EC and national mergers authorities. Pringle (HOP 29) observes that whereas EC legislation seems likely to make it more difficult for a large company to make a hostile takeover for another large EC company, national governments are likely to monitor closely how EC legislation will treat friendly mega-mergers which would be unacceptable under national laws and regulations. So far as the UK is concerned, the more pressing matter is whether a complementary EC Directive embodying a code of conduct governing transfers of corporate control will lead to the destruction of self-regulation through the Takeover Panel and its replacement by rigid statute law which could make the takeover timetable dependent on tactical litigation. This would not be unwelcome to those who consider that contested takeovers are treated too leniently, but delay would be associated with uncertainties which could well be against the interests of shareholders, although perhaps welcome to management and employees.

7 Criticism of Present Policy

I Criticism of Policy Aims

Much of the criticism of the aims of policy towards mergers and takeovers is focussed on the concentration of government concern on maintaining competitiveness. As pointed out in Chapter 6 Section II, the official defence of this position is that, whatever adverse effects takeovers may have on the promotion of other policy aims, this is not an argument for seeking to promote such aims through further restrictions on takeovers. In one important respect, there is no way of resolving the debate because none of the parties concerned appear to agree on the relative priority to be given to the various components of economic policy and are noticeably vague about the 'trade-off' between one policy and another. Nevertheless, it is important for us, in seeking to devise our own policy stance, to consider some of the criticisms of the allegedly narrow view taken by the Government.

Regional policy is one particular example which frequently provokes debate about competing policy priorities. It does so, firstly, because many contested takeovers involve regionally-based companies as the target – the Rowntree/Nestlé case being a good illustration – and, secondly, because of lack of symmetry between the criteria used by the OFT in deciding whether or not to recommend reference and the public interest issues which the MMC requires to consider once reference has been made. The very fact that Section 84 of the Fair Trading Act requires MMC to "have regard to the desirability of maintaining and promoting the balanced distribution of industry and employment in the UK" implies legislative recognition of the validity of concerns expressed when regional takeovers are in prospect.

It is often contended that this latter component of the public interest is not taken as seriously as it should be. Thus the Scottish Development Agency (see their Memorandum to the Trade and Industry Committee of the House of Commons, HC 229-i, p.95), in going over the same evidence as ourselves (see Chapter 5) about the growing dependence of Scottish industry on decision control outwith Scotland, has claimed that this erodes the development potential of Scotland and thereby is incompatible with long-term national economic development. We accept that takeovers could have adverse effects on regional growth and possibly contribute to a concentration of ownership which could have adverse effects on national prosperity, but we do not think that the evidence points towards the institution of a new regional dimension to takeover policy. There are two reasons for coming to this conclusion. The first has been indicated in Chapter 5 above. However important regional disparities in income and employment may be as evidence for a positive regional policy, the explanation of such disparities cannot be developed solely with reference to the takeover phenomenon. Indeed, a careful review of the evidence which takes account of the 'counterfactual' position, i.e. what might otherwise have happened to incomes and employment had a takeover not occurred, produces no clear link between the relative economic position of a region and the incidence of takeovers. Interestingly enough, the SDA itself rules out greater political interference in controlling takeovers and mergers and supports the present MMC case-by-case method. It goes further and suggests that there is no need for an increase in the number of referrals to MMC, concluding that "it is the policy framework that should be examined, to increase the emphasis on the long term competitiveness of the UK economy" (ibid.). This points towards our second reason for supporting the Government's view that regional policies need not embody some special provision about takeovers. We hope to show that important changes in *general* takeover rules and in corporate governance might help to reduce the loss of regional expertise and skills. Thus, while we accept the Government's view that the aims of regional policies may be achieved without embodying some special regional measures affecting takeovers, that is not to say that its existing methods for achieving these aims should be left untouched.

Terms such as 'the balance of income and employment' mask the fact that policy aims are to be judged by their effects on individual citizens for, in the last analysis, 'companies' are not sentient beings who benefit or suffer from the actions of government. This is clearly recognized in government statements which refer to the interests of shareholders and consumers. There appear to be no bones of contention between the Government and those organisations who make representations on behalf of individuals as spenders and savers about the attention given to their aims. The National Consumer Council (NCC), for instance, "believes that a strong competition policy is of vital importance to consumers" (HC 226–i, p.113). They part company with the Government over the prosecution of policy, a subject to which we shall return shortly. This is not so, however, in the case of individuals as employees, other than top management.

It is claimed by a number of those offering evidence, and notably the TUC, that employees' interests are not sufficiently recognized in the Government's policy aims The general argument for recognizing that employees have rights which should be protected in the case of takeovers runs something like this. While it is true that labour contracts, like debt contracts, are a prior claim on the earnings of a company, whereas shareholders only have a residual claim, shareholders, unlike employees, can cover their risks by spreading their capital across assets with different degrees of riskiness and can buy and sell assets swiftly, albeit at a cost, in order to adjust their portfolio. The fortunes of employees, on the other hand, are tied, at least in the short run, to the fortunes of the employing company. In the longer run, if they seek alternative employment as a way of reducing risk, they face much larger relative costs which may include retraining and relocation. The TUC (See HOP 18, p.40 et.seq.) has a natural concern for the interests of employees. In a full analysis of takeover activity which makes it clear that it is not opposed to takeover activity as such, it argues forcibly for the proposition, amongst others, that "the regulatory authorities should take account of whether a merger will be in the interests of employees of the firm, or firms" (HOP 18, p.47).

We regard it as rather surprising that the DTI makes no mention of this aim, even if only to dismiss it as not considered relevant or in order to claim, as in the case of 'other grounds for reference' considered above (See Chapter 6 Section II), that employees' interests are better protected by other policy measures.

Our view is that we are bound to consider employees' interests as a matter of expressed public concern. Accordingly, we shall look at some of the proposals made by the TUC and others when we present our own recommendations.

A third criticism of official policy points towards the narrow view taken of the threat to the economy from the exercise of economic power. It is argued that the motives for takeovers are more complex than simply the pursuit of profit alone, and that these motives are themselves harmful both because of their economic consequences and their manifestation in acts of dubious morality which give business a bad name. A forthright statement supporting this position came from the Finance and Ethics Groups of the Centre for Theology and Public Issues (CTPI) of Edinburgh University: "too often the motive for a takeover is not the industrial logic of the case but rather the greed, ambition, and desire for empire building on the part of one or more businessmen who enjoy the power game but are heedless of the wider human consequences of their actions" (HOP 27, p.7). Mr. Justice Henry in pronouncing sentence in the Guinness trial was even more forthright:

> The vice with which we are dealing is the corruption of commercial life. We are dealing with the problem against the background of the climate of the City in 1986: contested takeovers were referred to as "battles" – the metaphors of war were invariably used to describe them. In such takeovers, the stakes are high, the pressures intense, and the rewards of success potentially corrupting. The danger is that, when men are hell-bent for victory, greed is in the saddle and ordinary commercial probity and the law are thrust aside in the rush. The individual voice of conscience will not be heard.

Such statements highlight the activities of predators, but bidders certainly do not monopolise practices of doubtful morality and possible illegality, as is evident from some of the practices commonly used in resisting bids (cf. Chapter 2 above).

There are two separate issues raised by this concern. The first is the condemnation of the pursuit of power and the practices to which it gives rise. Even if there is a widespread feeling that condemnation is justified, it is not easy to imagine that governments can do much about eradicating power complexes. As the CTPI itself observes: "you can't make people good by legislation" (HOP 27 loc.cit.). The second is how this pursuit of power is manifested in the takeover process. It might reasonably be claimed by the Government that the proviso that takeovers must not restrict competition is sufficient to ensure that the consequences of greed and ambition are not detrimental to the performance of the economy. It is an empirical matter whether or not government measures act in the way that they are intended to, and a competent analyst can devise suitable methods of appraisal of the Government's actions.

Our view is that the question of the ethics of business and particularly of takeover activities must be a matter for public concern, and this Report has already examined some of the practices which have given rise to this concern. However, we do not wish to become drawn into a discussion leading to recommendations about the ethics of business which would take us far beyond the particular business practice of takeover. This is a highly contentious area, and it is by no means certain that there could ever be agreement as to which particular brand of ethics should govern business practice and how far it would be desirable or possible for the Government to impose it. (The David Hume Institute has commissioned a separate study by Professor Norman Barry which will be published shortly as a Hume Paper, and the interested reader of it will soon discover the force of our observation.)

Nothing in what we have said is meant to convey the impression that we have a completely neutral view of dubious takeover practices. Many of the objections to these practices are associated with the 'agency problem' (See Chapter 4 Section III) which offers the temptation to actors in the takeover drama to play with other people's money. Later in this Report we shall justify proposals which are designed to restore or reinforce the link between ownership of assets and control over them. Such proposals have the object *inter alia*, of containing even if they cannot eliminate some of the more objectionable practices which have given rise to public concern.

To conclude our analysis of the aims of merger and takeover policies, we have acknowledged that criticisms of the Government's position have some substance and that it pays insufficient attention to matters of public concern other than restriction of competition. While this means that we shall consider a wider list of aims than that identified by the Government when we come to offer our own recommendations, we accept that our principal interest coincides with that of the Government, namely the effect of takeovers on long-term performance.

Accordingly, the next part of our review of Government policy concentrates on the question as to whether the Government's policy instruments are those appropriate for the realisation of the policy aims which it prefers to pursue.

II   The Ambiguity in the Meaning of Competition

As we have observed in Chapter 6, the Government has attempted to define competition in legal terms by two criteria which put companies in the category of those suspected of being able to control their market. These are the 'Assets Criterion' and the 'Market Share Criterion'. However, it would be unfair to suggest that these are regarded as anything more than a starting point for much more sophisticated argument about individual cases. The question whether or not a merger will act to the detriment of consumers requires detailed investigations of such factors as control over price and quality of existing products and prevention of entry of suppliers who can offer lower prices for such products or new, improved products. The Reports of the MMC are replete with examples of careful elaboration and application of advanced economic analysis of competition.

Nevertheless, there is clearly dissatisfaction with the way that the Government perceives the application of the concept of competitive markets to takeovers. Not sufficient attention, it is claimed, is given to considering whether or not the *pre-conditions* for the successful operation of competition are fulfilled. There are three pre-conditions in particular which have come to the fore in the takeover debate.

The first pre-condition is that the competition 'rules' should be uniformly applied. In the case of takeovers, this can be taken to mean that no company could obtain an advantage over another company as a result of 'proof against bidding' devices. By implication, so it is argued (see Section III below), either there can be no immunity against takeover of a public company or the rules governing immunity against takeover must be the same for all.

The second pre-condition is that buyers and sellers compete on 'a level playing field'. The factors which might make the playing field uneven are many and varied, but a particular point has been made about the importance of differential tax treatment of companies and individuals in the capital market which produce a bias in the takeover 'market'.

The third pre-condition is that the property rights over the goods or assets which are bought or sold should be clearly defined. In the case of takeovers, the problem to which this gives rise is the link between ownership of assets of a company and control over their use. In a paper of fundamental importance for this Inquiry, Jonathan Charkham (See Charkham, 1988) has employed Hirschman's distinction between Exit and Voice to examine the options open to shareholders in exercising their control over company assets. 'Exit' in the form of the right to sell shares, i.e. to transfer the title to the assets of a company, is a readily available option, though the individual shareholder may face considerable costs in effecting a transfer. (One of the possible attractions of selling shares to a bidding company in a takeover is that these costs are much lower than those obtaining in ordinary share transactions which do not involve a change of ownership and control of a company.) The exercise of Voice is another matter, for this can normally only be exercised through the shareholders' representatives, that is to say the Board of Directors whom shareholders elect. The 'accountability' of directors to shareholders will clearly depend on the structure of corporate governance and how far it generates the incentive for shareholders to exercise their rights. In arguing, as the Government has done (see Chapter 6 Section II above), that a takeover or the threat of it is an essential way for disciplining management, then the implication is that the use of Voice alone is ineffective. This is to accept, however, that nothing can be done to improve corporate governance. As it has been put by Charkham: "It is argued that the threat of takeover is essential as a discipline because in practice investors have renounced the use of Voice. This proposition can however be turned upside down. If takeovers were more difficult or impossible would not investors be more inclined to use Voice as an instrument for improving poor management? Takeovers, in other words, are the lazy way out. Even if at the moment they are the only way, they are expensive and founded in monstrous illogicality – that a change of ownership is necessary in order to change management".

It is important before we turn to our own recommendations to look closely at these doubts about the completeness of the Government's competition policy as the guiding force in determining whether or not takeovers are in the public interest. At the same time, we must neither pre-judge the Government's stance nor assume that all the proposals for influencing the Government to alter it are acceptable.

III Uniform Application of Competition Rules: Bid Proofing

A frequently expressed complaint by British firms, particularly those threatened with takeover, is that whereas foreign bidders for British companies are free to bid, the reverse is rarely true. Foreign governments condone the use of all kinds of protective devices, ranging from widespread investment by German banks in domestic companies to restricted voting rights for certain classes of shareholders, which make it virtually impossible for British firms to mount contested bids against foreign companies. Such protective devices are also employed by British companies and, as Sykes shows (HOP 23, p.30), when privatisation of major public utilities is complete, bid-proof companies will be over one-third of the FT-Actuaries All-Share Index.

The complaint against the Government is that it deliberately encourages investment by overseas companies through its benign stance in relation to bid-proofing. Moreover, it exacerbates the problem by bid-proofing privatised companies through the retention of a 'golden share'. Surely, it is held, this is in contradiction to its own declared policy of supporting takeovers as devices for improving managerial efficiency. Futhermore, if a bid-proof company acquires companies and does not operate them efficiently, it is immune from the discipline of the takeover threat.

It cannot be claimed that the Government has ignored this problem.

In fact, one of the main sources of information on the very practices complained of is the Consultative Document on Barriers to Takeovers in the European Community issued by the DTI in January 1990. However, the Government is faced with a dilemma, at least in regard to bid-proof foreign companies. On the one hand, given its strong support for the view that takeovers have beneficial effects on the performance of the economy, it cannot countenance recommendations from representative bodies of industry that barriers should be erected against overseas bidders for corporate control of British companies. As the DTI state in their evidence (HOP 18, p.38): "Some have suggested that the way to 'level the playing field' is to reduce the opportunities available for foreign firms to acquire UK companies. The Government believes that this would be a mistake and that the proper way to tackle the problem of discriminatory treatment is not to erect one's own barriers but to seek to reduce or eliminate the barriers erected by other countries". On the other hand, it has to admit (See HOP 18, p.39) that the scope for tackling barriers which are derived from the structure of corporate governance in overseas countries obliges it to challenge the rationale of business cultures which in some fundamental respects are very different from our own. In consequence the Government has understandably pressed hard for a system of EC merger control which is competition-based. (For further discussion see DTI evidence in HOP 18, pp.37–38 and Robert Pringle's research report for the Inquiry, HOP 29.)

Our own view is that the Government is right to resist playing tit-for-tat with overseas Governments by placing major restrictions on overseas takeovers. Apart from the need to maintain the competitive principle which we have justified in earlier discussion (See Chapter 4 Section II), UK companies do benefit from the opportunities available to expand through direct overseas investment or through acquisition of companies in the US. However, this is not to be taken as an admission that we are convinced by the proposition that takeover or the threat of takeover is a necessary condition for maintaining if not improving the performance of companies.

IV   'The Level Playing Field': Tax Policies

One of the major problems encountered in attempting to run a mixed economy is the co-ordination of policy instruments. A particular instrument, such as a tax measure, which incorporates in its design incentives to achieve a certain result such as encouraging industrial investment, may have unintended effects on the attempt to achieve other policy aims. Two examples of particular relevance to mergers and takeovers have been brought to our attention.

The first example concerns the tax treatment of pension funds. Pension fund holdings of equities in 1988 were £110bn., a figure representing just over 50 per cent of the total equity holdings of financial institutions and

30 per cent of all listed UK and Irish equities. As pointed out in Chapter 1, the relatively generous tax treatment of pensions takes the form of the deductibility of pension premia by both employers and employees for tax purposes and the virtual exemption of accumulated occupational and personal pension funds from both income and capital gains tax. This treatment is of long standing and now Personal Equity Plans (PEPs) offer freedom from both income and capital gains tax on equity investments up to £6,000 p.a. In contrast, life insurance premia no longer attract relief for income tax purposes and savers who choose to invest directly are not eligible for tax relief, other than through PEPs.

The point at issue here is that tax treatment biases the savings market towards the channelling of funds through institutional investors who are alleged to take a short term view (Cf. Chapter 4 Section VI) and/or to respond to below-average performance by companies in which they invest simply by selling out. This frequently-made charge has been encapsulated in the words of Mr. Allen Sykes (HOP 18, p.15): "By their own frequent admissions, they (institutional investors) seldom exercise direct influence on companies and do not provide the resources or expertise to do so. If a company underperforms, their usual response is to reduce or eliminate their investment, leaving the task of change to their successors or to the board concerned. In sum, they are largely absentee owners who prefer to sell out when performance fails".

A more specific point about tax privileges was made to us by the Association of Investment Trust Companies (See HOP 18, p.14–15). In 1988, a bid was made by the British Coal Pension Funds for TR Industrial and General (TRIG), the largest general fund within the ITC sector. The Association argued that this amounted to a situation where the fiscal privileges awarded to pension funds were being abused, and, moreover, such a trend would lead to concentration of the management of investment into the hands of those who took a purely opportunistic short-term view of the market prospects of companies. The AITC argued that the 'opportunistic attention' given to ITCs arose primarily from the fact that the corporate structure of an ITC usually tends to produce a gap between share prices and net assets.

Clearly, the fiscal privileges afforded to pension funds are designed to fit with a well-established policy of encouraging saving for retirement. Whether this is the best way to achieve that aim is not our concern. It is also difficult to see why there need be any necessary connexion between fiscal privileges of this kind and the prevalence of 'short-termism' in fund management. The charge of 'short-termism' has been extended to institutional investors as a whole irrespective of their fiscal position. While it may be possible to criticise successive governments for not being able to create the economic climate which encourages long-term investment which would counter 'short-termism' (See Chapter 4, Section VI), it is hardly a logical conclusion to base any change in the fiscal regime of financial institutions which invest personal savings purely on the supposition that on occasions their operations have supported takeovers. This is not to say that such institutions should not behave in a responsible manner as intermediaries between personal savers and the capital market, and there may be other ways in which they might be encouraged to do so which would affect their attitudes to takeovers.

The second example is more directly concerned with the influence of tax law itself on the market for corporate control. The important general point to be made is that tax law is not designed as an instrument for controlling takeover activity in parallel with competition policy conducted through the MMC or the Takeover Panel. For example, the tax treatment of exchange of shares on takeover, of calculations of depreciation of transferred assets, and of the carry-over provision for tax losses could play a major part in influencing the scope and direction of takeovers. In fact, shareholders receiving shares in exchange of shares in the course of a merger are not subject to capital gains tax on the exchange, though the tax will be imposed when the exchanged shares are sold and with reference to their orginal cost. Assets transferred on takeover from the acquired company to the successor company are not deemed to have been realised for tax purposes and calculations of depreciation allowances for tax purposes are unaffected by transfer. While there are legal restrictions preventing companies from being purchased solely for the purpose of 'capturing' tax losses, normally tax losses can be carried over and used by the successor company.

Mr. John Chown, the well known expert on company taxation, has drawn our attention to three 'problem areas' in tax law which influence the market for corporate control.

The first area relates to past tax treatment of profits. Until the reform of the corporation tax in the 1970s, the two-tier profits tax system penalized dividend payments to shareholders and encouraged retention of profits in the business. As a result, the capital market became grossly distorted as the judgement of shareholders on which companies offered them the best prospects was impeded by lack of cash distributions. Retention of profits to avoid tax was justified by many pundits as a way of raising the level of industrial investment, but the removal of the 'market test' encouraged expansion of business by acquisition without regard to long-term prospects of the taken-over concerns as part of a merger or conglomerate. The process of takeover was precipitated further by the 'confiscatory' personal tax rates affecting the owners of private companies, who were thereby induced to sell to public companies as a way of realising their investments without incurring severe tax obligations. Certainly, considerable reductions in personal tax rates after 1980 and other tax changes have reduced the incentives to realise assets of private companies through sale to public companies.

Chown's point is that, whereas the tax regime has changed markedly to remove the bias towards merger formerly caused by the tax system, "old habits die hard: company managements are still very reluctant to disgorge surplus cash for reinvestment by their shareholders" (HOP 26, p.6). He also points out that "some of the past tax-driven conglomerates still exist as a rag bag of unrelated businesses. These need to be broken up into more manageable, stand-alone units. Institutional and tax factors continue to inhibit this economically desirable process" (HOP 26, p.8).

The second area of concern follows from the first. If Chown is right, then the economic logic followed by the present Government would require that the tax system should not inhibit the process of demerger. It is true that in 1980 the newly-elected Government did permit companies to demerge without incurring tax penalties but nothing like the 'positive discrimination' in favour of mergers has been instituted.

The third area of concern identified by Chown is presented by the 'prejudice problem'. The problem arises out of the UK system of Advance Corporation Tax (ACT) which requires companies to pre-pay an amount equal to the credit granted to shareholders for that part of the corporation tax on the profits underlying the dividend distribution. This creates several problems for UK companies, particularly those incurring losses but continuing to pay dividends out of reserves. When a UK company earns a substantial part of its profits abroad, the ACT represents an onerous burden if the company relies on these profits for distributions to its UK shareholders. It will get a credit for the tax paid to foreign governments under double taxation agreements but will have to pay ACT based on the whole dividend payment whatever the country of origin of the profits. This 'prejudices' its position if it cannot meet its dividends out of its UK taxed profits. Consequently, it offers a strong tax incentive for international companies to 'buy' UK source profits, not because such acquisitions are better profit earners at the margin, but because of the distortion produced by the tax laws. Chown quotes a number of cases. The 'prejudice' problem is only one example of ways in which the tax laws encourage particular forms of takeover which could not be justified on the efficiency grounds supported by the Government. Until the 1984 Finance Act abolished fast write-off of capital investment, companies with large capital investments with more allowances than they could use as claims against taxed trading profits, became the target of predators of profitable companies which were not capital-intensive. Mergers could therefore 'buy in allowances' as a way of reducing their tax obligations and increasing post-tax profits. The ability to carry forward tax losses incurred by the Rover group was a major factor in the inducements offered to British Aerospace to take it over (For further intriguing details, see Chown, HOP 26, pp.15–18).

The post-war history of the tax treatment of companies, insofar as it has a bearing on the market for corporate control, suggests that the tax authorities have adopted a reactive stance. Successive reforms of the system of profits and income taxes have been designed to promote such objectives as maintaining revenue yields necessary to finance government services, and the use of tax policy as a stabilization device to control the levels of investment, consumption and employment, subject to the same regard for maintaining incentives to save, invest and to work. The simultaneous achievement of such objectives by even a wide range of different tax measures is very difficult if not impossible, and there is continuing controversy amongst academics, professional tax accountants, administrators and business associations about the priority to be given to different aims, and how taxes affect the economic variables that they are designed to influence. The standard of debate has risen markedly following the Meade Report published by the Institute of Fiscal Studies in 1978, but many issues concerning the appropriate mix of tax instruments to fit with these (largely macro-) objectives remain unresolved. It is therefore not surprising if the added problem of the use of tax measures in order to promote 'a level playing field' in the market for corporate control is not referred to in official discussion of mergers policy. The tax authorities were not directly represented on the Liesner interdepartmental group which produced the Blue Paper on Mergers Policy. The possible distorting effects of taxation on mergers and divestments is not mentioned in either the Blue Paper itself or in the DTI evidence presented to our Steering Committee. One must assume that the official view is that it is a secondary matter which it should be possible to cover by 'tidying-up' operations when tax policies come under review.

It would be easy for us to leave the matter there and not get involved in a difficult and recondite area of official policy. It is quite possible to put forward suggestions for some changes in tax law which would supplement other measures designed to improve the market for corporate control, and we shall mention a few of these. The problem is that the scope of our Inquiry cannot allow us to investigate whether any of these design changes would have side effects which would make other objectives more difficult to achieve. We are well aware that the revenue authorities will take as their point of departure their perceived duty of 'protecting the revenue'. Consequently, the reader should not be surprised if our proposals (Chapter 8) regarding taxation are characterized by more circumspection than others which we shall put forward.

V Corporate Governance and Corporate Control

As was stressed earlier in this chapter (Section I), if the Government's main aim in competition policy is to improve companies' economic performance, then a *prima facie* case could be made for policy measures which support the opportunity to change the management rather than the ownership of a company. The criticism is frequently made that the Government has favoured the latter at the expense of the former.

As Professor Jack shows (HOP 31), the general approach of British company law is still very much that enunciated in the Jenkins Report of 1962 (Report of the Company Law Committee, Cmnd1749, 1962), namely that the law should "avoid, as far as possible, placing obstacles in the way of honestly and fairly conducted takeover transactions". As we have seen in Chapter 6, apart from the overall control of takeovers exercised by competition policy, non-statutory regulation by the Takeover Panel has been designed to ensure that 'honesty and fairness' prevail. Further evidence of the Government's penchant for facilitating takeover is to be found in the underlying thesis of the DTI Consultative Document, Barriers to Takeover in the European Community, which is that other member states place obstacles in the way of takeover which do not exist in the UK. The actual and potential 'barriers' extend far beyond those associated with competition policy, an area in which the latest EEC Directives clearly accord with British practice (see Chapter 6 Section II).

An interesting and important example is provided by the issue raised in the DTI document concerning the identification of shareholders. As already pointed out (Chapter 6 Section III), UK practice requires that details of shareholders are freely available to the public and that such information can be obtained easily, e.g. through centralised registration undertaken by the central government. Disclosure of beneficial ownership is based on a threshold reduced from 5 per cent to 3 per cent as a result of the Companies Act, 1989. The DTI's concern is that even where in other countries there is registration of shareholdings, the share registers may not be available for public inspection. The clear interest of the Government is that incomplete disclosure and difficulty of access to information is an important barrier to takeover. Professor Jack maintains that the original reason for a system of disclosure was to act as an 'early warning system' for the directors of the target company. The combination of a system of disclosure and mandatory bid provisions "very often puts a company irreversibly 'into play' irrespective of the intentions of a substantial stakeholder" (HOP 31). He adds: "It is an odd irony that a system expected initially to be of help to the directors of target companies may have turned out to be of such assistance to the potential offeror that its absence is regarded as an important barrier to the bidder."

Whether or not an 'early warning system' favours one side or another in a hostile bid, the present stance of the Government towards takeovers and the Takeover Code hardly encourages directors of a target company to pursue the alternative of improving the management structure. Such improvements cannot be instituted overnight, whereas the official stance, including that of EC, favours almost an indecent haste in the prosecution of a bid. Directors can derive little comfort from MMC procedures, for even if some delay is inevitable during official scrutiny of a bid, they must know that the large majority of bids are allowed to go ahead. The defensive measures allowed to targets, once a bid has been made (cf. Chapter 1 Section IV) are restricted both by the law and, more specifically, by the Takeover Code. An appeal to shareholders to remain 'loyal to the company' may have little chance of success when shareholders compare the (inevitably) tentative forecasts of the gains which might accrue to them in the future, against the substantial premia over the pre-bid price of shares which could be immediately on offer.

This last point raises a crucial matter. How might shareholders be persuaded that the company would be better to change its management structure rather than be submitted to takeover? In a British context this would effectively mean close contact and understanding between large institutional investors and companies. Only in this way could a situation be anticipated where management structure could be quickly adapted to satisfy shareholders that it was in their long term interests not to sell out. However, selective provision of information to major shareholders for that purpose comes up against the restraints on insider dealing forbidden by the Companies Securities (Insider Dealing) Act 1985, which makes it a criminal offence to recommend or to procure others to trade on the basis of inside information. Not only the company issuing the shares but its major shareholders could be committing a criminal offence. The law is backed up by the provisions of the Takeover Code that information provided to shareholders must be full, accurate and public. Therefore, as Professor Jack stresses, "there is little wonder then that at least some fund managers seek to distance themselves from the company and refuse to attend briefings even after publication of their company's results when the state of knowledge of the directors and investors should most closely coincide" (HOP 31). Without shareholder pressure, the directors have no effective way of using a change in management structure as a way of improving managerial performance and thereby keeping shareholders happy.

The above criticisms are only meant to offer a broad outline of the lines of criticism made of current policy and only relate to issues concerning shareholders' rights and company behaviour which concern companies' economic performance. Within the context of this discussion it would be wrong to suggest that the Government is not aware of and has not considered these arguments. This can be clearly shown by reference to the wide brief of the Takeover Panel (See Manser (HOP 21) and the Consultative Document on Barriers to Takeovers in the European Community (DTI 1990), particularly Annex A.). If one accepted the Government's view that takeovers are an integral part of the competitive process and, subject to safeguards considered in Chapter 6, work towards the improvement of economic performance, then one might go a long way towards accepting the present thrust of policies. However, because we contend that the evidence does not support the Government's claim that takeovers are a necessary condition for achieving that end, we are bound to adopt a critical stance towards the present legislation and regulations on corporate governance.

Our review of suggested changes and our own recommendations form a major part of the discussion in the following chapter.

8 Recommendations

I Background

Our Inquiry is at one with successive Governments in accepting that
the achievement of 'workable' competition in both product and factor
markets has played and will continue to play an important part in bringing
our economic performance more into line with that of major industrial
countries. Clearly, upon such performance depends the growth in the
availability of resources necessary to improve standards of living all round
and in the quality of life. However, the results of our Inquiry do not buttress
the confidence that the Government places in the workings of the market
for corporate control as a key element in the efficient creation and use
of assets. The existing methods of surveillance of corporate takeovers,
principally through competition policy and self-regulation, are imperfect.

We have demonstrated that, for a variety of reasons, the market for
corporate control does not display important characteristics which would
ensure that the outcome would accord with economic efficiency.

The first reason for this is that there are biases in the system which discriminate in favour of takeovers, especially of smaller companies by larger
ones: for example, tax incentives such as the 'ACT trap', the application of
certain accounting rules which conceal the role of acquisitions in corporate
performance, and the requirements of the Stock Exchange Listing Rules
which which impose for listed companies more onerous requirements, in
terms of information to be given and the need for shareholder approval,
the bigger an acquisition is in relation to the acquiring company.

A second reason why the market for corporate control may not be
efficient is that although share prices on the London Stock market may
well adjust quickly and fully to available information (these prices are
'information-arbitrage efficient'), there has to be doubt about whether or
not these prices reflect the present value of future cash flows ('fundamental-
valuation efficiency'). If the stock market undervalues shares in this sense
(as it apparently did, for example, in the takeover of Rowntree by Nestlé)
then takeovers will be stimulated to take advantage of the discrepancy,
even where that takeover may do little or nothing in itself to enhance
wealth creation and may in the long run impair it.

The third reason for doubting the efficacy of the market for corporate
control follows from the decline of the private shareholder and the growing

divorce between ownership and control. This separation means that the principal direct participants in the takeover process – the management of the companies, the institutional shareholders and the various advisers and facilitators involved – are not playing with their own money and there is a risk, at least, that their interests and those of the eventual owners may diverge.

For all these and other reasons there has to be doubt about whether the 'free' market will, in fact, discriminate satisfactorily between those takeovers which are in the interests of maximising economic welfare and those which are not. Resources would have been wasted, but damage would be limited, if competition in product markets were always sufficiently vigorous for companies which had grown overwhelmingly large or had over-diversified were rapidly forced by market pressures to divest ill-advised acquisitions. In fact, there is evidence in the growth of corporate divestments that exactly this is happening, but it may not always happen without considerable delay. When it does, much of the original vitality and innovative skill of the once independent concerns that have been taken over may have been lost.

It seems to us equally obvious that the system of corporate governance and the nature of product competition in the UK are not in themselves always sufficient to ensure that the best available management is in charge of all companies. Indeed if it were, then the Government would not be able to claim, as it does, that the threat of takeovers is a necessary discipline on incumbent management. Takeovers are not necessarily the only or even the most effective way of reforming management, as experience in the successful economies of FR Germany and Japan, where hostile takeover bids have been rare, plainly demonstrates.

The comparison between the UK and Germany and Japan is revealing because it helps to put the problem of takeovers into perspective. In the course of this Inquiry, and in particular in studying experience in other countries, we have reached the conclusion that large takeovers (and especially hostile bids) are merely a symptom of a deeper problem. This problem is that much of the energies of our business people is being diverted from building businesses by product innovation and internal expansion, their traditional strengths, and into the pursuit of short-term profitability and growth by acquisition. However, this is not a problem that can be solved by tighter legislation on takeovers.

Freedom to expand by acquisition is essential and takeovers undoubtedly have played an important part in the success of many large businesses, particularly in expansion into new markets at home and overseas. Takeovers also play a useful role in the orderly contraction of capacity in declining industries. Equally, however, many internationally successful companies – Rolls Royce Aero, Shell, IBM and BMW, for example – have made little use of takeovers. Some large takeovers have undoubtedly promoted wealth creation, others perhaps not; but we are very sceptical of the ability of the MMC or any other body, *ex-ante*, to discriminate between the two. We therefore do not consider that the answer lies in further major tightening of the investigation and control procedure for takeovers.

Whilst takeovers are not necessarily a bad thing and there are strong forces in favour of them (Chapter 3), it is nevertheless important not to encourage them. We recommend below, therefore, that major biases in favour of takeovers in public policy should be investigated and, as far as practicable, removed. We consider it particularly important that measures should be taken to remove biases in favour of the separation of ownership and control, and also that competition should be promoted by removing as far as possible remaining barriers rather than by negative intervention in the takeover process which, by interfering with the workings of the market, would inevitably not only incur hidden costs but would, by failing to deal with the root causes of the problem, be ineffective.

We are not confident that rapid results will flow from the actions we propose, or indeed that all of them can ever be implemented without considerable delay. The undue emphasis upon short-term considerations in the UK economy is deeply rooted in our culture and has long and complex historical causes. This culture cannot be changed overnight. We also recognise that our freedom to act directly on some of the matters dealt with is limited by our obligations within the European Community and the need to take account of actions by governments and business in other countries.

We do not expect that our analysis of the causes of and remedies for the anxieties created by the recent boom in takeovers (which will surely recur again at some point in the future even if action is begun now) will command immediate agreement among all those that have submitted evidence to us. Most of what we conclude, however, with one notable exception, is echoed by one or more of the parties involved in the debate, and we hope that the synthesis that we put forward will command respect if not agreement. For example, The Association of Investment Trust Companies drew attention to "the incompatibility between the Government's stated commitment to encouraging wider share ownership, and the fiscal privilege enjoyed by institutions" (HOP 18). The University of Edinburgh Centre for Theology and Public Issues takes the same view that we do, that a central issue is '...the fact that the real owners – the shareholders – are largely passive and do not exercise the responsibilities which come with ownership'. Practically all the evidence received supports, as the Association of British Insurers puts it, 'the concept of a free market in corporate control' (HOP 18). The TUC argue that 'The takeover boom is a reflection of the short-termism that pervades British industry' (HOP 18), and we have offered evidence which supports their position.

What we did find totally missing in the evidence submitted was any reference to the crucial importance for competition and wealth creation of the removal and prevention of the erection of barriers to the entry of new firms. This is not surprising because new entrants are, by definition, not represented among the interest groups in society. It is all the more important, therefore, that their crucial role should not go unrecognised and unsupported by government.

In the next section of this final chapter we review briefly some of the principal recommendations made to us and explain why we have not adopted them. In a final section we put forward those recommendations which we do accept and some other, more radical proposals that we put forward ourselves in line with our belief that it is the underlying problem rather than takeovers themselves which needs to be addressed. We have not elaborated any of our proposals in detail, and all will require detailed consideration. We are therefore involved in an attempt to persuade the authorities that the issues surrounding takeovers are part of a wider problem concerning the thrust of industrial and economic policy. It is for this reason that we envisage our contribution to the search for remedies as that of re-defining the context in which policy changes should be made. Until that context is understood and its relevance agreed upon, there seems little point in making elaborate and detailed proposals.

II   Review of Some Submitted Proposals

We are now in a position to itemize the criteria for judging the relevance and the effectiveness of proposed policy changes affecting takeovers. These are:

i)   **An increase in the relative importance of owner–management in commercial and industrial life and in the stability and pro–active nature of shareholder involvement in corporate control.** This criterion is the positive counterpart to our previous criticisms, which many others have voiced, about the 'agency problem' (see Chapter 4 Section IV above).

ii)   **A change in emphasis in competition policy towards reducing barriers to entry as a means for increasing the potency of competitive forces.** Competition policy should become judged not simply by its actions to control mergers already in existence or contemplated, but also by the stimulus given to new entrants by process and product innovations to challenge the market position of established companies, the latter objective being in our view much the more important of the two.

iii)   **The adoption of a position of neutrality towards rather than bias in favour of takeovers.** It is, of course, difficult to measure the extent of 'bias' but our review of the evidence above (see Chapter 5 Section II) indicates that present government policies take a benign view of the takeover process based on rather doubtful evidence of its effects on economic performance (see Chapter 4, Section VII).

iv)   **The avoidance of new distortions resulting from modifications, in or additions to, regulation of takeovers.** One of the major arguments against the use of regulatory measures to influence and to control the operations of companies is that they divert scarce professional resources into negotiation between government and industry. This is in addition to the diversion of resources into the 'manufacture' of takeovers in the interests of market-makers.

We do not regard it as our task to review all the recommendations put to the Inquiry or under general discussion. It is sufficient, as an introduction to our own proposals, to exemplify how the criteria would act as a sorting device for the kind of recommendations commonly advanced.

We consider, first of all, proposals which fall within the general area of *competition policy*, offering two prominent examples. Thus, it is claimed that even if the Government confines its review of corporate takeovers primarily to effects on the degree of competition, takeover bids falling within the scope of the Government's size criteria (see Chapter 5, Section III) should be automatically examined by the OFT and that the onus of proof that bids are in the public interest should rest with the bidder. We understand the logic of these proposals. If, for example, the market capitalisation of a company is in excess of £1b, as Mr. Sykes (HOP3, p.55) suggests, this could offer prima facie evidence that it is either bid-proof or in a position to indulge in monopolistic practices which might only be revealed by detailed investigation. The Blue Paper on Mergers Policy (DTI 1988) conceded that there were two main possible advantages of some mandatory form of pre-notification along the lines found in other countries: "it can be used to prevent mergers being completed before the authorities have an opportunity to investigate", and "it can be linked to a requirement to supply relevant information" (*op.cit.* p.12). The TUC recommends that "a requirement on bidding companies to provide prior justification for their takeover plans is an integral part of an effective regulatory framework" (Evidence in HOP 18, p.40 and 62). Our own view, like that of the other participants in this discussion, can only be based on what we hope is an informed judgement. A comprehensive and equitable system of pre-notification combined with automatic referral would require a large increase in investigatory resources and would therefore not be compatible with our fourth criterion. Even then, it might not achieve the desired result, because it would either mean that the government would review a substantial number of cases which, in the end, required no action or it would force the government to 'second-guess commercial judgments' (cf. Chapter 5, Section IV) in a larger proportion of bids and with no certainty that it or its statutory agencies would have guessed right. However, in accepting the Government's present view, we do so bearing in mind our other criteria, and particularly criterion (ii) which is not at present an integral part of official competition policy.

Our second example under the heading of competition policy concerns bid-proofing. This matter was discussed in Chapter 7, Section III with particular reference to the perceived advantages of overseas companies in the bidding process. This would follow from the ownership systems in Japan and Continental Western Europe which inhibit the operation of attempts to gain control of companies through the stock market. We can reject one set of remedies rightaway. Companies should not be allowed to protect themselves from bid-proof overseas predators by recourse to such devices as cross-shareholdings, restriction of the voting rights of particular classes of shares, 'poison pills' and the like. As Mr. Sykes has put it: "the general argument for bid-proofing is misplaced. It would substitute the possibility of management abuse as a remedy against the alleged ills of many hostile takeovers but who can say the cure would be preferable to the disease?" (HOP 23, pp.36–37). On the contrary, there is a strong case for non-discrimination against overseas companies, even if they are bid-proof, if the result is to increase competition and to promote inward investment. Of course, if the result of a bid were to restrict competition, then this would presumably make it a prima facie case for investigation by the OFT and/or EC under the new dispensation.

We are more sympathetic to the view that the UK Government could do more to persuade overseas governments to open up their markets to takeovers from UK companies. For example, the Association of British Insurers (ABI) made a particular point of the opportunities which should be available for overseas expansion by the British insurance industry and which are frustrated by bid-proofing devices in European countries. ABI concludes: "we suggest that it is imperative that the UK Government should exert the utmost endeavour to persuade its EC partners to amend their legislation, regulations, accounting rules and other market practices in order to move more closely towards the UK system of handling corporate takeovers, in which decisions are essentially taken in the market place on the basis of the fullest possible information being provided to shareholders and potential investors" (ABI Evidence, HOP 18, p.7). While we support the emphasis in such a statement on the opening up of markets to competition, we are sceptical about the reception of EC countries to an approach from our Government which extols UK values and practices. As it is, some of these practices cannot be shown to improve our economic performance. We are satisfied that the Government has taken on board the importance of an attack on such barriers through a competition-based merger control system operating through EC, but we must emphasise once again that our own support for the Government's position presupposes that it take a much wider view of the scope of competition policy.

The second area of policy change is corporate governance and would point towards further **changes in company legislation**. We received a number of proposals for the re-design of the relations between shareholders, directors and managers with a view to the removal of 'short-termism' as a governing factor in company decision-making.

There is, for example, a substantial body of opinion in the UK which favours a major extension of the role of non-executive directors. The argument is that these directors could help to check possible conflicts of interest between executive directors and shareholders and could, for example, be specifically charged with expressing an opinion on the shareholders' interests in proposed mergers. The proponents of this view have in mind the continental practice of separate executive and supervisory boards. Professor Shaw, for example, favours a two-tier board structure as one possible solution to the present difficulties. He comments:

> The supervisory board provides a close-knit group to which executive management can report in detail and with which they can share both plans and concerns, and at the same time acts as an effective instrument of management supervision and control. Looking outward to the shareholders whose interests they serve directly and unequivocally, members of the supervisory board act both as a filter of detailed information and as a conduit for the expression of individual concerns of shareholders and managers. I would therefore recommend urgent re-examination of the supervisory board structure for British companies. In the short term, I would recommend the International Stock Exchange require the appointment of at least one-third of the Board of listed companies as non-executive with a minimum of (say) three, as a step towards effective shareholder supervision and managerial accountability. Such non-executives could be given specific responsibilities (by the Takeover Panel) to comment on merger proposals – either as bidder or target.

In the normal British case, the non-executive directors are nominated by the executive directors and sit together on the same board, and we are doubtful both of their real independence and of the wisdom of mixing up supervisory and executive functions. However, if non-executive directors were themselves substantial shareholders or represented specific shareholders, which is usually not the case in Britain, then an enlargement of their role would meet our criteria for approval and should be encouraged.

It has also been argued that the independence of auditors should be increased by prohibiting them from supplying non-auditor services such as consultancy to their audit clients, and by obliging frequent rotation. These proposals, which are under consideration following draft EC Directives, have little to do with the takeover issue, and the only comment we should wish to make is that if implemented, small and medium sized companies should certainly be exempt. The separation of auditing, book-keeping and other functions carried out by accountants for smaller firms would raise costs already inflated by the unnecessary requirement for compulsory audits in closely held companies.

Finally, we also reject calls for **changes in taxation (and also company law)** intended to limit the voting rights and after-tax gains of short-term shareholders. The motives for these proposals are certainly consistent with our desire to increase shareholder commitment but would do little to increase it and represent an undesirable restriction of freedom. A return to the distinction between long and short term capital gains in the UK would complicate the tax system and stimulate the emergence of evasion devices, both highly undesirable, and tend to reduce the already insufficient level of liquidity in market-making in all but alpha stocks.

III The Inquiry's Recommendations

As we have continually emphasised, corporate takeovers are more a symptom of the major defects in the working of the free market system than a principal instrument for ensuring that it works efficiently. We have offered plenty of evidence that this is a correct interpretation of the British situation. Therefore, if the market is to work in a manner which is to improve economic performance we have to formulate proposals which remedy these defects rather than concentrate on tinkering with legislation with a view to restricting takeovers. In other words, we must demonstrate that there are policy alternatives which, though they do not restrict takeovers unnecessarily, make corporate takeover a less attractive option as a means for making companies operate more efficiently.

It could be argued that, within the time-scale in which policy changes could be agreed, decided upon and implemented, the capitalist system would adjust on its own towards the renaissance of proprietor-capitalists. If, as our evidence suggests, corporate takeovers frequently do not lead in the longer run to an increase in the profitability of firms, individual shareholders with large holdings may feel impelled to take a more direct interest in management. However, even those who, like the editor of *The Economist*, Rupert Pennant-Rea, (Supplement to *The Economist* 5th May 1990) have emphasised that capitalism is very good at changing itself (which is why all the obituaries are about communism!), do not assert that the 'invisible hand' will be able to guide the system unaided back to the path of economic advance from which government induced distortions have led it. We agree and for that reason offer a detailed list of recommendations which we believe are in keeping with the end in view. Our recommendations do not deal directly with the regional issues discussed in Chapter 5, for the reasons explained there. However, we believe that the policies which we propose, to remove biases in favour of takeovers and to promote new entrants, will be of benefit to the regions. Indeed, there is already some evidence that the Government's general policies in the past ten years are more likely to reduce regional inequalities than the specific regional policies which were pursued earlier. In the same way, whilst we have not made specific recommendations on the ethics of takeovers, we believe that our proposals, taken as a whole, will help to minimise the temptations to adopt unethical practices which bring financial dealings into disrepute.

i) **Our prime recommendation is that the Government should begin immediately to work towards the removal of tax discrimination between different forms of saving.** The ultimate objective should be to make the tax system neutral as between direct and institutional investment in equities, unit trusts, investment funds and other securities on the one hand, and bank, building society and other deposits and investments in property or other assets, on the other. Investment by owner-managers in their own business should receive equal tax treatment to that given to investment in domestic property or large company securities, for example.

How this objective should be achieved is a matter for consideration and debate. Complex questions of equity, the promotion of self-provision for old age, administration, evasion and other matters, will need to be answered. (For detailed discussion, see Chappel, Kay and Robinson 1990.) The Government has already declared itself in favour of tax neutrality, has removed discrimination in favour of life assurance and has allowed tax relief on interest on domestic property borrowings to be eroded by inflation, but continues to introduce new measures (PEPs, TESSAs) which despite good intentions, create new distortions in favour of institutional investment.

A bold move towards tax neutrality for savings would meet all four of our criteria. It would encourage directors of large companies to commit more of their savings to the acquisition of shares in the companies they manage, instead of in property or in the shares of other large companies via institutions; it would, more generally, promote direct private share ownership (another declared government objective) and it would encourage a further shift in resources towards small firms. By reducing, or at least reducing the growth of the share of savings under the control of financial institutions, tax neutrality would reduce some of the biases in the system in favour of takeovers that we have identified (Chapter 3). Finally it should result in a considerable simplification of the tax system and would improve 'tax transparency', both of which are desirable on other grounds.

ii) **The Stock Exchange and competing interests should undertake a review designed to promote the use of lower tier markets and to reduce dealing costs for private investors.** 'Big Bang' and other changes following the Financial Services Act of 1986 have led to higher dealing costs for private investors, and these and share price weaknesses have snuffed out the bottom tier of unlisted securities markets. These changes have further discouraged long-term investment by private shareholders and raised barriers to entry. Our tax proposals will help.

iii) **The Government should carry out a comprehensive review of barriers to entry in all sectors of the economy.** These barriers are both specific to sectors and of general application: for example, legislative protection of monopolies and quasi-monopolies in auditing services, gas and electric power, and general government measures which raise the costs of entry for smaller firms. One example of these barriers which falls into both of these categories is the compulsory audit mentioned above. The Government also needs to look again at the unnecessarily high levels of compliance cost in various forms of regulation from financial regulation to business taxation which bear harmfully upon the smaller firm.

iv) **Accounting standards should embody more disclosure of the contribution of mergers to financial performance.** Future profits growth can be flattered by acquisition accounting with heavy provisioning and depreciable asset write down. Immediate profit growth is provided by merger accounting which recognises profits earned before acquisition. As an illustration of the accountancy profession's desire to contribute to more responsible accounting, we refer those interested to a publication of the Institute of Chartered Accountants of Scotland, *Making Corporate Reports Valuable*. These issues are now firmly on the agenda of the new Financial Reporting Council and Accounting Standards Board. We hope they can make progress in eliminating the worst excesses of misleading accounting practices which tilt the odds in favour of a bidder. We agree with the proposal by Mr. Allen Sykes that all quoted companies should be required to publish annual audited figures of investment per share broadly defined. We also agree with his suggestion that some changes to the accounting methods used by fund managers might help alleviate the pressure they are under for short-term performance.

v) **We recommend, as suggested by the National Consumer Council, that monitoring of both contested and uncontested mergers should be instituted, particularly with a view to ascertaining whether or not guarantees or undertakings given to the work forces of target companies have been honoured.** We realise that bid documents are formulated to sell takeover proposals and are not contractual statements, and that guarantees of future employment will normally be vaguely formulated because of uncertainty about future business prospects. The only sanction that monitoring would offer would be exposure to public criticism. The NCC would assign the general monitoring function to the MMC, but we consider that the Takeover Panel is the more appropriate body. The Panel's Rule4 requires a bidding company to state its intentions with regard to a range of matters concerning the future of the offeree company. It is more important from our point of view, that, in following this Rule, companies should be obliged to state their intentions regarding, above all, the organisational structure as well as the continued employment of the employees of the offeree company and of any of its subsidiaries.

vi) **Remaining biases in favour of acquisitions under existing tax legislation should be reviewed and, as far as practicable, removed by the Government.** Serious consideration should be given to the abolition of corporation tax in the long term. We appreciate that such a measure would now require agreement at the level of the European Commission. Corporation tax not only introduces distortions into the takeover process, but it leads to the waste of very significant resources in compliance and reduces tax transparency. The fiction that companies have an identity distinct from that of their owners and customers serves no useful purpose in taxation, however shocking the suggestion that it should be abolished may be in some quarters. Of course, it goes without saying that such a radical step would require careful examination of the revenue implications of abolition and the substitution of alternative forms of taxation which would not produce other distortions might be difficult to avoid.

vii) **Takeovers are often an expensive and inappropriate way of replacing poor management. We welcome indications that institutional shareholders** are taking a more positive interest in the composition of boards of directors, as advocated by the Association of British Insurers, and hope that the institutions acting separately or collectively will follow this policy, and as a first step see that the PRONED Code for non–executive directors, which is supported by the CBI and all major city interests, is put into practice.

viii)   British banks have never been so deeply involved with their commercial customers as those in Germany and Japan, and we do not think it would be desirable for them to attempt to be so even if it were practicable. Over-protection can impair flexibility. That said, we can see advantages for all parties if leading bankers' relationships with their customers were deeper and did not preclude some element of longer term investment which, we believe, would have a stabilising influence.

ix)   The London International Stock Exchange should reduce the bias in the rules which discriminates in favour of the acquisition of smaller companies (those below the Super Class One Category, see HOP 24, p.53–54). For example, these rules at present operate in a way which requires shareholder approval for a takeover of any of the top 100 quoted companies by one of the top 20 of these companies, but not for the acquisition of any company outside the top 100 by one of the top 20.

x)   We recommend only one other change to the regulatory framework as proposed by Professor E. Victor Morgan: that the concept of competition in the Fair Trading Act should be broadened to include other aspects of market power than market share and pricing policy. This would enable references to be made to the MMC on wider grounds than those permitted at present. Once a reference has been made, the matters listed under Section 84 of the Act are probably sufficiently broad to allow full consideration of all the important issues, but the change we propose should stimulate the Commission to broaden the scope of its inquiries. We do, however, urge all of those concerned with regulation to take account of innovative record in assessing the genuine existence of competitive conditions.

We would not be averse to some emphasis being placed on the work of the MMC on the regional impact of takeovers though we have found no evidence that takeovers have had adverse effects on the overall economic performance of regions. In any case, our recommendations, taken as a whole, by making takeovers less attractive, should allay some of the fears of those who deplore the attraction of regional business talent to the South East as a result of the re-location of company headquarters. There is surely something in the argument that, if this is happening on a large-scale, then overall economic performance might suffer. This is perhaps a matter that requires careful investigation on its own by the DTI.

xi)   Changes to our own regulatory system, and indeed our broader recommendations on taxation and other matters, will need to take into account developments at a European level. The Government should attempt to influence these developments in the directions that we have proposed. It is important that the activities of the Competition Directorate should be free from political interference and that it should be a separate agency.

We recognize that it is easy to fall into our own trap by offering goals to reach but no description of the path to reach them and no time scale. We are also well aware from previous experience that we may be implicitly underestimating the difficulties of implementation, including both the regulatory and revenue changes which would be bound to be required. It is beyond the scope and resources available for this Inquiry to pursue these matters. What we have offered are what we believe to be cogent reasons why the present thrust of policy discussion on takeovers has taken a wrong turning by the emphasis placed on more and more regulation by Government and self-regulation by the City. This is to let the Government off the hook, because, as we have seen in Chapter 7, the Government can easily produce good reasons why a cure in the form of further regulation would be worse than the disease. What has been missing in the present discussion is the forging of the link between diagnosis and cure. There is clear evidence that the 'agency problem' manifested in the divorce between ownership and control of business and in the institutionalization of shareholding reveals a major defect in our free market system. The first stage in solving it is to set a new agenda for policy discussion. Our recommendations are designed to fulfil that exacting task.

References

Works Quoted in Part I

Auerbach, Alan J., (Ed) *Corporate Takeovers: Causes and Consequences*, University of Chicago Press, 1988.

Bannock, Graham, *The Takeover Boom: an International and Historical Perspective*, Hume Occasional Papers, No.15, The David Hume Institute, Edinburgh, 1990.

Bannock, Graham, *Taxation in the European Community*, Paul Chapman Publishing, 1990.

Bannock, Graham, *The Economic Impact of Management Buy–Outs*, 3i (Investors in Industry), 1990.

Bannock, Graham, *Britain in the 1990s: Enterprise Under Threat?*, 3i (Investors in Industry), 1991.

Bannock, Graham, *Small Business Policy in Europe*, The Anglo-German Foundation, forthcoming.

Bannock, Graham and Peacock Alan, *Governments and Small Business*, Paul Chapman Publishing, 1989.

Berle, Adolph A., and Means, Gardiner C., *The Modern Corporation and Private Property*, Revised Edition, Harcourt Brace, 1967.

Chandler, Alfred D. Jr., *Scale and Scope*, Harvard University Press, 1990.

Chown, John, *Taxation and Mergers Policy*, Hume Occasional Papers, No.26, The David Hume Institute, Edinburgh, 1991.

Cooke, Terence E., *Mergers and Acquisitions*, Blackwell, 1986.

Davis, Evan, and Bannock, Graham, *The Nestlé Takeover of Rowntree*, Hume Occasional Papers No.30, The David Hume Institute, Edinburgh, 1991.

Fairburn, James A., and Kay, John, (Eds), *Mergers and Merger Policy*, Oxford, 1989.

Freeman, Christopher, *The Economics of Industrial Innovation*, Second Edition, Frances Pinter, 1982.

Hannah, Leslie, *The Rise of the Corporate Economy*, Methuen, 1976.

Hart, P.E., and Clarke, R., *Concentration in British Industry 1935–75*, Cambridge University Press, 1980.

Jewkes, John, Sawers, David and Stillerman, Richard, *The Sources of Invention*, Second Edition, Macmillan, 1969.

King, Mervyn A., and Fullerton, Don, (Eds), *The Taxation of Income from Capital*, University of Chicago Press, 1984.

Lawrie, T.M., *Whose Business are Business Mergers?*, 1990.

Morgan, E.Victor and Morgan Ann D., *The Stock Market and Mergers in the United Kingdom*, Hume Occasional Papers, No.24, The David Hume Institute, Edinburgh, 1990.

Morgan, E.Victor and Morgan Ann D., *Investment Managers and Takeovers: Information and Attitudes*, Hume Occasional Papers, No.25, The David Hume Institute, Edinburgh, 1990.

Porter, Michael, *The Competitive Advantage of Nations*, Macmillan, 1990.

Prais, S.J., *The Evolution of Giant Firms in Britain*, Cambridge University Press, 1976.

Scitovsky, Tibor, *Welfare and Competition*, Irwin, 1951.

Scott, John, *Capitalist Property and Financial Power*, Wheatsheaf Books, 1986.

Utton, M.A., *The Political Economy of Big Business*, Martin Robertson, 1982.

Works Quoted in Part II

Ashcroft, Brian, Love, James, and Scouller, James, *The Economic Effects of The Inward Acquisition of Scottish Manufacturing Companies*, ESU Research Paper No.11, Industry Department, Scottish Office, Edinburgh, 1987.

Ashcroft, Brian, and Love, James, *Corporate Takeovers and The Interests of Regional and Local Communities*, Hume Occasional Papers, No.17, The David Hume Institute, Edinburgh, 1990.

Bannock, Graham, *The Takeover Boom: An International and Historical Perspective*, Hume Occasional Papers, No.15, The David Hume Institute, Edinburgh, 1990.

Blaug, Mark, *The Methodology of Economics or How Economists Explain*, Cambridge Surveys of Economic Literature, Cambridge University Press, 1980, Chapter 5.

Charkham, Jonathan, "Corporate Governance and The Market for Control of Companies", Bank of England Panel Paper No.25, March 1989.

Cosh, Andy, Hughes, Alan and Singh, Ajit, *Takeovers and Short–termism in the UK*, Industrial Policy Paper No.3, Institute for Public Policy Research, London, 1990.

Department of Trade and Industry, "Evidence" in *Hume Occasional Papers*, No.18, The David Hume Institute, Edinburgh, 1990.

Elliot, Gerald, *Mergers and Takeovers: Short and Long–Term Issues*, Hume Occasional Papers, No.14, The David Hume Institute, Edinburgh, 1989.

Gowland, David, *Finance and Takeovers*, Hume Occasional Papers, No.20, The David Hume Institute, Edinburgh, 1990.

Hall, P., and Pickering, J. F., *The Determinants and Effects of Actual Abandoned and Contested Mergers*, University of Manchester Institute of Science and Technology (mimeograph)986.

Hughes, Andy, "The Impact of Merger: A Survey of Empirical Evidence for the UK", in Fairburn, J., and Kay, J. A., (Editors), *Mergers and Merger Policy*, Oxford, 1989.

Jensen, Michael, "Takeovers: Their Causes and Consequences", *Journal of Economic Perspectives*, Volume 2 No.1, 1988.

Limmack, Robin, *Takeover Activity and Differential Returns to Shareholders of Bidding Companies*, Hume Occasional Papers, No.19, The David Hume Institute, Edinburgh, 1990.

Meeks, G., *Disappointing Marriage: A Study of the Gains from Mergers*, Cambridge University Press, 1977.

Morgan, E. Victor, and Morgan, Ann, D., *The Stock Market and Mergers in the United Kingdom*, Hume Occasional Papers, No.24, The David Hume Institute, Edinburgh, 1990.

Morgan, E. Victor, and Morgan, Ann, D., *Investment Managers and Takeovers: Information and Attitudes*, Hume Occasional Papers, No.25, The David Hume Institute, Edinburgh, 1990.

Newbould, G. D., *Management and Merger Activity*, Guthstead, Liverpool, 1970.

Office of Fair Trading, "Evidence" in *Hume Occasional Papers*, No.18, The David Hume Institute, Edinburgh, 1990.

Reid, Gavin, *Efficient Markets and the Rationale of Takeovers*, Hume Occasional Papers, No.22, The David Hume Institute, Edinburgh, 1990.

Richardson, Ranald, and Turok, Ivan, *Scotland for Sale? The Impact of External Takeovers in the 1980s*, Strathclyde Papers on Planning No.15, University of Strathclyde, Glasgow, 1990.

Rowley, Charles, and Peacock, Alan, *Welfare Economics: A Liberal Restatement*, Martin Robertson, London 1975.

Scottish Financial Enterprise, *Hostile Bids and Investor Loyalty*, Edinburgh, 1989.

Scottish Office, "Evidence" in *Hume Occasional Papers*, No.27, The David Hume Institute, Edinburgh, 1990.

Sykes, Allen, *Corporate Takeovers: The Need for Fundamental Re-thinking*, Hume Occasional Papers, No. 23, The David Hume Institute, Edinburgh, 1990.

Tobin, James, "On the Efficiency of the Financial System", Lloyds Annual Bank Review No.2 (Edited by Christopher Johnston), London, 1989.

Works Quoted in Part III

Association of Investment Trust Companies, "Evidence" in *Hume Occasional Papers No.18*, The David Hume Institute, Edinburgh, 1990.

Barry, Norman, *The Ethics of Business*, Hume Paper No.18, Aberdeen University Press for The David Hume Institute, Aberdeen, (forthcoming).

Charkham, Jonathan, "Corporate Governance and the Market for Control of Companies", Bank of England Panel Paper No.25, March 1989.

Chown, John, *Taxation and Mergers Policy*, Hume Occasional Papers, No.26, The David Hume Institute, Edinburgh, 1990.

Department of Trade and Industry, *Mergers Policy* (Blue Paper), Her Majesty's Stationery Office, London, 1988.

Department of Trade and Industry, "Evidence" in *Hume Occasional Papers, No.18*, The David Hume Institute, Edinburgh, 1990.

Department of Trade and Industry, *Consultative Document on Barriers to Takeover in the European Community*, Department of Trade and Industry, London, 1990 (mimeographed).

Director General of Fair Trading, "Evidence" in *Hume Occasional Papers, No.18*, The David Hume Institute, Edinburgh, 1990.

Edinburgh University Centre for Theology and Public Issues, "Evidence" in *Hume Occasional Papers, No.27*, The David Hume Institute, Edinburgh, 1990.

Institute of Fiscal Studies, *The Structure and Reform of Direct Taxation*, (Report of a Committee chaired by Professor James Meade), Allen and Unwin, London, 1978.

Jack, Robert, *Takeovers: How Level a Playing Field does Company Law Provide?*, Hume Occasional Papers, No.31, The David Hume Institute, Edinburgh, 1991.

Manser, William, *The UK Panel on Takeovers and Mergers: An Appraisal*, Hume Occasional Papers, No.21, The David Hume Institute, Edinburgh, 1990.

Morgan, E.Victor, *Economic Issues in Merger Policy*, Hume Occasional Papers No.5, The David Hume Institute, Edinburgh, 1987.

Morgan, E.Victor, *Monopolies, Mergers and Restrictive Practices : UK Competition Policy 1948–87*, Hume Occasional Papers No.7, The David Hume Institute, Edinburgh, 1987.

Pringle, Robert, *Takeovers and the EC*, Hume Occasional Papers, No.29, The David Hume Institute, Edinburgh, 1991.

Sykes, Allen, *Corporate Takeovers – The Need for Fundamental Rethinking*, Hume Occasional Papers, No.23, The David Hume Institute, Edinburgh, 1990.

Trade and Industry Committee, House of Commons, *Memoranda of Evidence*, HC 226–i, Her Majesty's Stationery Office, 1991.

Trades Union Congress, "Evidence" in *Hume Occasional Papers, No.18*, The David Hume Institute, Edinburgh, 1990.

Appendix Evidence Presented to the Inquiry

During the course of the Inquiry, nine studies of different aspects of the takeover phenomenon were commissioned and the results were published in the Institute's Hume Occasional Paper series. These are:

The Takeover Boom: An International and Historical Perspective, by Graham Bannock, HOP 15.

Corporate Takeovers and the Interests of Regions and Local Communities, by Brian Ashcroft and James H. Love, HOP 17.

Finance and Takeovers, by David Gowland, HOP 20.

The UK Panel on Takeovers: An Appraisal, by William Manser, HOP 21.

Efficient Markets and the Rationale of Takeovers, by Gavin C. Reid, HOP 22.

The Stock Market and Mergers in the United Kingdom, by E. Victor Morgan and Ann D. Morgan, HOP 24.

Investment Managers and Takeovers: Information and Attitudes, by E. Victor Morgan and Ann D. Morgan, HOP 25.

The Control of Mergers and Takeovers in the EC, by Robert Pringle, HOP 29.

The Nestlé Takeover of Rowntree, by Evan Davis and Graham Bannock, HOP 30 (to be published in May 1991).

In response either to direct invitations or to advertisements in the Press, a number of individuals and organisations sent us written opinions and several of these were also published in the Hume Occasional Paper series. These are:

Mergers and Takeovers: Short and Long-Term Issues by Sir Gerald Elliot, HOP 14.

The Association of British Insurers, collected in HOP 18 *together with papers by:*

The Association of Investment Trust Companies

The Office of Fair Trading

The Department of Trade and Industry

The Trades Union Congress

Takeover Activity and Differential Returns to Shareholders of Bidding Companies, by Robin Limmack, HOP 19.

Corporate Takeovers: The Need for Fundamental Rethinking, by Allen Sykes, HOP 23.

Taxation and Mergers Policy, by John Chown, HOP 26.

The Scottish Office, collected in HOP 27 together with papers by:

The Edinburgh University Centre for Theology and Public Issues

Dennis Henry

Corporate Takeovers: How Level a Playing Field does Company Law Provide? by Robert Jack, HOP 31 (to be published in May 1991).

These published papers are summarised in the following pages. Copies of the full texts may be obtained from The David Hume Institute, 21 George Square, Edinburgh, EH8 9LD, telephone (031) 667 7004, fax (031) 667 9111. A complete set may be obtained at a discount of 10per cent on the prices noted at the head of each summary.

In addition to foregoing, the persons named below gave us opinions or drew our attention to work which they had published in the field of our Inquiry. Eighty five Investment Managers, whom it would be inappropriate to name individually, answered a questionnaire on their attitudes to and information about takeovers which Professor and Mrs. Morgan sent to them in the course of their research published in Hume Occasional Papers Nos. 24 and 25.

We wish to express our gratitude to all these persons and organisations and also to those who corresponded with us on various aspects of the Inquiry.

Mr. R.E.B. Atkinson, 60 Ashbourne Court, Woodside Park Road, London N12.

The Church of England's Board of Social Responsibility, Church House, Westminster, London SW1.

Mr. P.J. Corcoran, Prudential Insurance Company of America, Newark, New Jersey, U.S.A.

Mr. D.E. Erdal, Chairman, Tullis Russell, Markinch, Glenrothes, Fife.

Mr. R.S.G. Gill, The Old Cottage, St. James' Road, Netherbury, Bridport, Dorset.

Mr. M.I. Gillibrand, 7 Tal-y-Cae, Tregarth, Bangor, Gwynedd.

Mr. Gordon Hazzard, Gordon Hazzard Ltd., 5 Balfour Place, Mayfair, London, W1Y 5RG.

Mr D.F. Jamieson, The Institute of Chartered Accountants of Scotland, 27 Queen Street, Edinburgh.

Mr. H.W. Laughland, Higher Stratton, Stratton Chase Drive, Chalfont St. Giles, Bucks, HP8 4NS.

Mr. Martin Lipton, 299 Park Avenue, New York, U.S.A.

Mr. B.N. Lenygon, Highfield, Bells Yew Green, East Sussex, TH3 9AP.

Mr. E. McGivern, Inland Revenue, Somerset House, London, WC2 RLB.

Mr. A.G.C. Paish, Association of British Insurers, Aldermary House, 10–15 Queen Street, London, EC4N 1TT.

Mr. H.C. Petersen, 100 California Street, San Francisco, California, 94111, U.S.A.

Mr. Dick Taverne, Prima Europe Ltd., 10–12 Cork Street, London, W1V 5FB.

Dr. Ivan Turok, Lecturer in Economics, Centre for Planning, University of Strathclyde, Glasgow.

Mergers and Takeovers: Short and Long-Term Issues

Hume Occasional Paper No.14 £2.00

Contributed by Sir Gerald Elliot who is Chairman of the Trustees of The David Hume Institute and a well-known Scottish industrialist. He made his career with Christian Salvesen plc, retiring recently as its Chairman.

The basic elements of the takeover process and the effects, baneful and benign, attributed to that process are outlined. The motives and responsibilities of management in conducting the process and the subsequent difficulties of achieving successful fusion of differing corporate cultures are discussed. The stimulus to high performance supposed to be given to UK Companies by the threat of takeover is contrasted with the actual high performance economies of Germany and Japan, where hostile takeovers are almost unknown.

The paper examines the belief, held strongly in Scotland, that takeovers can lead to undesirable concentration of power regionally and nationally and bring adversity upon the societies concerned, and the fear that, post 1992, purely economic considerations will concentrate company power in the centre of Europe, draining away talent and power from peripheral regions and countries. This leads on to a discussion of Government's generally non-interventionist attitude to the takeover process and of the primacy accorded to the criterion of competition in the economy by the regulatory authorities. 'Yet it is clear that contested takeovers do not find general favour except with the shareholders of the target company, who get an unexpected windfall, or by the management of the bidding company which increases its importance and power. Most people see takeovers as potential sources of social and economic harm to their community..... We are all aware that a competitive market takes reasonable care of the proper short-term allocation of resources to create wealth. It is much less effective in dealing with longer term economics or with social issues'. Anglo-Saxon attitudes towards companies as ad hoc mechanisms for the delivery of wealth are contrasted with the views of the German and Japanese who see them as wealth-creating social organisms with their own history, culture and social responsibilities.

The author then develops his main thesis that 'in a healthy society, there should be multiple centres of independent economic power, well dispersed'. The 1973 Fair Trading Act lays down a series of criteria for the Mergers and Monopolies Commission to apply in considering the public interest, including that of 'promoting, through competition, the reduction of costs and the development and use of new techniques and new products, and of facilitating the entry of new competitors into existing markets' and of 'maintaining and promoting the balanced distribution of industry and employment in the United Kingdom'. The objects of these clauses could be achieved if the criterion of maintaining independent centres of economic activity were added to that of maintaining competition in the economy. This should apply principally in contested bids where the targeted company declares its wish to remain independent.

The author starts by recognising that mergers and takeovers are important elements in competitive capitalist economies and that regrouping by this process maintains the growth and profitability of individual companies. He concludes by stressing the responsibility of the Government to exercise a degree of control in the long-term public interest.

The Takeover Boom: An International and Historical Perspective

Hume Occasional Paper No.15 £4.50

A commissioned paper by Graham Bannock who is the Research Director of The David Hume Institute's Inquiry into Corporate Takeovers in the UK as well as being the Managing Director of the economics consultancy Graham Bannock & Partners Ltd.

The paper was commissioned to provide a preliminary statistical background for the Inquiry, covering the UK, USA, France, Germany, Japan and other countries over as long a period as feasible. After a section setting out definitions and sources, an analysis of trends in merger activity in the UK over the period 1954–1988 is followed by comparisons with activity in other countries over broadly the same period, and by a discussion of other dimensions of merger activity; those which come within the purview of regulatory authorities, divestments, cross-border activity etc.

The principal findings are as follows.

1. In number and money value, the recent wave of merger activity reached record height but, after allowing for inflation and the growth in GDP, the wave is not much greater than that of 1968.
2. Merger activity is more important in relation to GDP in the UK, USA and probably in Canada, than in France, Germany and Japan, though it is increasing everywhere. Mergers are getting larger, particularly in the UK. Hostile takeovers are more common in the UK and USA than elsewhere.
3. In the recent wave, UK industrial companies were devoting about 40 per cent of their total uses of capital to acquisitions, increasingly to acquisitions overseas. This is not much more than in earlier waves. The UK is spending more on acquisitions abroad than foreign companies are spending in the UK.
4. Buy-outs, buy-ins and other forms of divestment constitute an increasing proportion of acquisition activity in the UK, where it is more important than in France and Germany, though it is increasing there too.

In a concluding section of comment on the findings, the author touches on all the issues which give rise to public unease about takeover activity and thus he maps out the field of the Institute's Inquiry.

Corporate Takeovers and the Interests of Regions and Local Authorities

Hume Occasional Paper No.17 £4.00

A commissioned paper by Brian Ashcroft, Director of the Fraser of Allander Institute at the University of Strathclyde and James H. Love, Lecturer in Economics and Research Fellow in the Fraser of Allander Institute.

The paper was commissioned to pursue the requirement in the Inquiry's terms of reference to assess the consequences of takeovers in relation to economic efficiency and the public interest, having particular regard to regional and local community factors.

Part 1 gives the background to the concern about the effects of corporate takeovers on the performance of regional economies and presents data showing that while there is no simple north-south divide in takeover activity, the balance has been consistently in favour of companies headquartered in South East England.

Part 2 discusses the analytical problems posed by the introduction of a spatial, regional element into the economic examination of takeovers. The effects of takeover on acquired companies are analysed in terms of their impact on the nature and structure of the acquired firm's production rather than, more narrowly, on its performance. Better performance may be associated with a reduction in the scale and sophistication of its operations, which could have long-term effects on the wider regional economy. These effects may occur through changes in the acquired firms' structures leading to changes in demand for regional inputs; through direct competitive effects on other local economic activities and through intangibles such as the transfer of superior technical or managerial skills which may eventually diminish the regional resource base.

The result of the analysis indicates the following.

1. Externally-acquired companies suffer a loss of autonomy, not necessarily detrimental and usually offset by improved management techniques, financial control and access to investment finance. There is evidence of improved sales and access to new markets but mixed evidence on loss of employment through post-acquisition plant closures. As far as individual firms are concerned, the effects are mainly beneficial or neutral with only 20 per cent of cases being clearly detrimental.
2. As regards external effects on the wider regional economy, there is clear evidence of reduced linkage with local suppliers, particularly of suppliers of professional services and of loss of top management and key operational functions which could in turn lead to increased emigration and a lack of dynamism and entrepreneurship.

In a concluding chapter, the authors set out the policy implications of their research. They point to the recognition in the 1973 Fair Trading Act that in merger policy the regional interest forms part of the public interest, but that in deciding whether or not a qualifying merger should be recommended for referral to the Mergers and Monopolies Commission, the Director General of Fair Trading is not obliged to take account of the public interest criteria: these apply only to the MMC's own investigations. Thus in the administration of the Act, excessive weight is given to competition criteria in determining referral and insufficient weight is allowed to the Act's specific expression of the desirability of 'maintaining and promoting the balanced distribution of industry and employment in the United Kingdom'.

Evidence Submitted to the Inquiry

Hume Occasional Paper No.18 £6.00

At the commencement of the Inquiry a number of individuals and organisations were invited to contribute opinions to the Inquiry and, through advertisements in the Press, the public at large were also asked to make their views known. This paper contains five responses to these invitations.

The Association of British Insurers

The ABI supports the concept of a free market in corporate control as it currently operates in the UK. Insurance companies regard themselves as responsible investors rather than speculators but they owe a duty to their own policy holders and shareholders to assess each takeover bid on its individual merits. However, there is a strong tendency to support existing managements, and they seldom sell to a raider.

Dealing with the frequently-made suggestion that, rather than relying on the stimulus of the threat of takeover, institutional investors should themselves become more directly involved in shaking up slack managements, the ABI point out that this in fact happens more frequently than is apparent to the outside world. In cases where a single insurance company has a large shareholding, it may act alone or with one or two partners: in other cases there may be joint action, including action with other categories of institutional investors.

On cross-border takeovers, ABI is not satisfied that the playing-field is level vis a vis European and Japanese companies and it advocates that, as 1992 approaches, the UK Government should press its EC partners to assimilate their practice to the more open UK system, and that the MMC should be required to take more specific account of international competition rather than merely competition within the UK itself.

The Association of Investment Trust Companies

The paper describes the role of Investment Trust Companies and the trend towards increasing specialisation within this sector.

In the market for corporate control they are both investors and victims. As investors, ITCs are generally willing to invest a proportion of their assets in high risk or longer-term ventures and some Trusts – the so-called Merchant Venturers – specialise in doing so. Their spheres of operation include takeovers, buy-outs and buy-ins. They are liable themselves to become victims of takeover when their share prices trade at a discount to their underlying assets. The case of British Coal Pension Fund's bid in 1988 for TR Industrial and General is cited as bringing to a head a number of issues of concern to the investment trust industry and to the structures of the savings market as a whole. These include the declining influence of the private investor, the effect of the fiscal privileges enjoyed by institutions on wider share ownership, the concentration of fund management into fewer and larger hands, and the fact that, irrespective of size or performance, ITCs may become the victims of tax-exempt institutions 'in order to satisfy the insatiable appetite of faceless institutions and opportunistic arbitrageurs for quick profits.'

The Office of Fair Trading

This is a purely descriptive note which starts with the fundamental statement that 'Merger policy in the UK is largely a part of competition policy' having as its primary objectives:

a) to identify and prevent mergers that reduce competition in the UK market;
b) to allow other mergers to go ahead with the least possible delay or impediment.

A sketch of the historical background of merger control is followed by outlines of the statutory and policy frameworks within which the control is operated. The different rules of the Director General of the Office of Fair Trading (to advise), the Secretary of State for Trade and Industry (to decide) and the Mergers and Monopolies Commission (to investigate) are described. It is noted that while the MMC has a duty to take a wide view of the public interest 'merger policy is not intended to act as a surrogate for regional policy or industrial and social policy.'

The method of establishing the jurisdiction of the controlling bodies is described (target assets of £30m + or 25 per cent market share) and the factors taken into account in the analysis of competition are listed. National and international aspects are reviewed with emphasis on the irrelevance of considerations of nationality to the competition analysis. Similarly, regional and local aspects are considered in the context of competition and it is emphasised that 'It is not current policy to refer (to the MMC) solely because a merger might have some detrimental economic effect in a region e.g. the move of operations from one part of the country to another.'

The paper ends with a note on recent changes in control procedures.

The Department of Trade and Industry

This paper complements that of the Office of Fair Trading. It starts with a statement that, 'in general, the market should be allowed to decide whether a merger should go ahead .... So the Government should only intervene in those mergers in which the private interests and the public interests diverge.' It sets out the legal basis of the control machinery and states that 'the main public interest issue to be considered when deciding whether to refer a merger to the MMC is the potential effect on competition in the UK.' In elaborating this statement it explains the concept of the 'relevant market' in which competition is to be safeguarded in the public interest.

The paper then goes on to consider other grounds of reference to the MMC : a) regional or local effects, b) foreign takeovers of UK companies, c) leveraged bids and d) the research and development factor. On a) it states Government believes regional issues are best addressed by other regional policies, not by mergers policy. On b) it states that it is in the interests of the UK economy that there should be as little official interference as possible in the two-way flow of inward and outward investment but raises the issue of reciprocal freedom in the country of a potential foreign acquirer of a UK company. On c) it maintains a non-interventionist stance but perceives a potential danger to the public interest in a high degree of leveraging. On d) it is wholly non-interventionist.

After sections on the changes in procedure introduced in the 1989 Companies Act and on the interaction of statutory merger control procedures and the City Takeover Code, the paper then discusses the European dimension, welcoming the fact that the EC Merger Control Regulation sets up competition-based criteria as the main grounds for EC investigation. It describes the interaction between the UK and EC merger control systems and recent initiatives to remove barriers to takeovers in EC.

The Trades Union Congress

The paper recalls the TUC's submission to the Liesner review of merger policy of 1986 which called for a requirement that bidding companies should provide prior justification for their takeover plans, for a wider definition of public interest, for more effective monitoring of claims and undertakings made by bidding companies, for prior consultation and information for trade union representatives and for measures to safeguard pension funds. These principles have since been reiterated by the TUC, most recently in 1989 when they also expressed concern about the distortion of bidding companies' performance caused by highly leveraged financing of takeovers.

In the course of a review of the UK policy framework, the paper claims that the primacy of the narrow competition criterion in deciding whether to refer a case to the MMC means 'that conglomerate bids .... are effectively outside any regulatory control.' It spells out the factors that the regulatory authorities should take into account in assessing the public interest: maintaining and promoting effective competition in so far as this is compatible with an international competitive capability and a positive balance of trade; promoting the interests of consumers, purchasers and environmental protection; encouraging, through competition, reduction in costs, new techniques and products and the entry of new competitors; being in employees' interests; maintaining production and output in the UK and securing national control of strategic industries. It recognises that this wider role would require more regulatory staff and advocates that the authorities should have the power to require an acquiring company to divest its acquisition if it fails to implement undertakings given in its offer.

The paper provides a review of trends in EC mergers and takeovers and discusses the EC Regulations and Directive under consideration at the time of writing. It suggests that the Transfer of Undertakings Regulations be used as a model for national legislation to implement the EC Directive on Takeovers. The TUC's prime concerns in this respect are about the automatic transfer of contracts of employment to the new owner and ensuring that dismissals directly related to a transfer are automatically deemed unfair.

The paper concludes with an expression of hope that the principles for a regulatory framework on the lines which the TUC put to the Liesner review as outlined above will be reflected in law and practice at European level.

Takeover Activity and Differential Returns to Shareholders of Bidding Companies

Hume Occasional Paper No.19 £3.00

Contributed by Robin Limmack who is a Senior Lecturer in Accounting and Finance in the University of Stirling. The paper is based on research financed by the Economic and Social Research Council and the Centre for Investment Management, University of Stirling.

The paper investigates the factors which might determine the success or otherwise of acquisitions as measured by the impact on the wealth of bidder company shareholders. 'Managerial theories of the firm suggest that a policy of corporate growth may be pursued even when such a policy is detrimental to the interests of shareholders'. Previous studies are extended by examining the factors influencing post-acquisition performance of UK bidders, in particular whether bad acquisitions are related to the pursuit of managerial objectives and whether bidders with superior performance records achieve superior acquisition-related returns.

The author describes fully his method of identifying and measuring bidder company performance and growth, the relatedness of the activities of bidder and target companies, profitability, target shareholder premium and other variables, and he presents the results of his analysis statistically.

He identifies 'a significant negative relationship between bidder growth and subsequent acquisition-related returns' which suggests that 'bad acquisitions are indeed related to the pursuit of managerial objectives'. He also finds that there is no 'unambiguous evidence that managements with superior track-records also achieve superior performance in acquisitions'.

The author adds a coda to his conclusions. He analysed the pattern of returns for two separate time periods – 1977–80 and 1981–86 – and found 'a significant difference in the pattern of returns between two sub-periods. The change in economic climate and regulatory framework appears to have led to an improvement in the efficiency of operations of the market for corporate control in the United Kingdom. There does also appear to be some as yet undetected relationship between the health of the economy and returns from acquisitions. Finally, the results obtained should provide a warning against reading too much into the findings of studies into security price behaviour using data extracted from relatively short time periods.'

Finance and Takeovers

Hume Occasional Paper No.20 £2.00

Commissioned from David Gowland who is a lecturer in Economics and Director of In-service Courses at the University of York.

The paper discusses the motives for takeover and then considers the impact and consequences of the means by which these are conducted, setting the discussion in the context of a more general argument about the theory of the firm. The neo-classical proposition that the goal of the top management is to maximise profits and share prices, subject to the avoidance of excessive risk, is contrasted with managerial theory that top management has discretion to pursue its own objectives even when these are in conflict with the interests of shareholders. Within this broader framework, recent economic analysis has focused on 'the market for corporate control.' Theories based on this analysis suggest that takeovers should lead to a rise in profitability. However, the evidence is that they rarely increase the underlying profitability but do increase stock exchange values. This leads to the proposition that the motivation of many mergers is financial, that is in the interests of the shareholders, without raising profits.

The author then elaborates the concept of the financial merger. Tax discrimination gives shareholders an incentive to seek returns in forms other than dividends. Although tax reform has reduced incentives to take over or to be taken over, yet the incentives still remain. The 'PE game' provides another motivation. Takeovers of smaller by larger companies constitute one way of profiting from anomalous differences in PE ratios. Takeover may also be a means of achieving an optimal debt:equity ratio.

Without denying the importance of other motives for takeovers such as 'managerial goals', the author argues that the evidence suggests that most are financially-motivated, by tax considerations, by stock exchange anomalies and by sub-optimal debt:equity ratios. He suggests that 'the effects of takeover and merger on corporate financial structures are amongst their most significant effects', one of which 'has been to put further emphasis on finance within companies' to the detriment of their operating functions.

The U.K. Panel on Takeovers and Mergers

Hume Occasional Paper No.21 £4.00

A commissioned paper by William Manser who is an economic and financial consultant, an author and an Associate of the Economist Intelligence Unit.

The paper describes the development of the UK Panel on Takeovers and Mergers from a City Working Party formed by the Governor of The Bank of England in the 1950s to a more formally constituted body which issued the City Code on Takeovers and Mergers in 1968 and grew to its present stature after the 1986 Financial Services Act added representatives of a number of the newly-created Self-Regulatory Organisations to the Panel's membership.

The Panel has a single function, that of ensuring the observance of the Rules of its Code, which has itself only a single object, namely that of ensuring fair treatment for shareholders in the course of a takeover operation. The Panel is not allowed to consider wider matters such as general economic and social policy or the merits of individual cases. The Rules of the Code are summarised and the ten General Principles on which the Rules are based are set down in full in an Appendix. The Panel's method of working is to monitor takeovers as they proceed. It offers advice on the Code to the participants in order to prevent breaches of the Rules rather than seeking to detect breaches by ex post facto review. Though the Code is not justiciable, the Panel has considerable non-statutory powers of enforcement and uses them.

The author examines the statutory alternative to self-regulation. He favours the system operated by the Panel but is opposed to any extension of its mandate to enable it to take into its purview interests wider than just those of the shareholders, for instance those of the employees. He discusses recent reviews of the effectiveness of the Rules which were conducted separately by the CBI and then by the Panel itself. He provides a short survey of the international dimension of the regulation of takeovers, in particular the European Communities' proposed 13th Company Law Directive which he fears may embody the Continental preference for statutory control rather than British-style self-regulation which he characterises as having the merits of speed, certainty, and flexibility, which bring many advantages to shareholders.

Efficient Markets and the Rationale of Takeovers

Hume Occasional Paper No.22 £4.00

A commissioned paper by Gavin C. Reid, who is a Reader in Economics in the University of Edinburgh.

The paper considers what efficient market theory can contribute to our understanding of takeovers. It starts from the contention that free markets are efficient even though participants normally pursue their own interests. It then introduces from games theory the attractively named concept of 'superadditivity' or, more prosaically, synergy; that the value of the union of two firms cannot be less than the sum of their respective values and may be more. There may be a 'positive value gap'.

The author then develops a theoretical discussion of the efficiency of the stock market, the methods of optimising the value of portfolios and the 'bubbles and fads' which distort the market. Under the rubric of agency effects he sees the market for corporate control as one of several market mechanisms which may reduce agency costs, thus increasing efficiency and he discusses a variety of defensive devices such as golden parachutes, shark repellants, poison pills, greenmail, capital re-structuring and the re-assignment of voting rights.

He concludes as follows. 'A fundamental postulate of the efficient market approach is that mergers and takeovers should be of benefit to both the target and the acquiring firm, or at least should leave neither worse off....Available evidence, of the event-study form, or otherwise, suggests the generic case has potential benefit for the target and zero benefit for the acquirer.....(T)he "superadditivity" condition seems to be violated quite frequently: more mergers and takeovers are being undertaken than can be justified by appeal to efficiency criteria.'

Corporate Takeovers – The Need for Fundamental Re-Thinking

Hume Occasional Paper No.23 £6.50

Contributed by Allen Sykes who was Managing Director of Consolidated Goldfields until it was taken over by Hanson in 1989 and who combines his current business activities with writing on economics and politics from a businessman's perspective.

The author states his main criteria for judging takeovers as:

1. to achieve the optimal use of corporate assets in Britain, regardless of the nationality of ownership, and of assets owned by British companies abroad;

2. to protect strategic firms and industries from foreign takeover whenever there is a strong public interest case, taking account of the general level of foreign domination of British business.

These criteria lead him to a discussion of the power vacuum at the heart of the existing system of corporate governance under which passive institutional investor ownership of some 80 per cent of equity capital fails to deliver 'constant and informed owner pressure for corporate efficiency'. He then evaluates the arguments of the 'protectionist' and 'market forces' schools of thought on takeovers and considers their proposed remedies for perceived defects. He concludes that the free Stock Exchange systems of English-speaking countries, which permit takeovers as a discipline upon inefficient management, lead to short-termism and to the under-valuation of British companies. This in turn attracts a disproportionate number of foreign takeovers. His ideal system would ensure that 'Directors would be under constant knowledgeable management discipline but would have the time, resources and incentives to ensure long-term corporate efficiency'. To this end, he makes a series of detailed recommendations based on the criteria stated above.

The OFT should be required to consider referring foreign bids for strategic companies to the MMC on public interest grounds.

The Government should restrict the use of bid-proofing devices.

The Government should review the terms of reference, practice and procedures of the OFT and MMC and ensure that they are adequately resourced.

The OFT should be required to examine all bids from larger bid-proof companies which are monopolistic or are operating inefficiently.

The Takeover Panel's compulsory 30 per cent bid-level rule should be reduced substantially.

Accounting measures should be taken to expose and deter short-termism and to highlight long-term investment.

Measures should be taken to develop performance-based incentive schemes for directors which involve financial penalties for non-performance.

The banks, the investment institutions and the representative business organisations should co-operate in studying Continental and Japanese corporate governance and banking practice with a view to improving British systems and, whilst the results of the study are being acted upon, the Government should impose a short, selective moratorium on hostile takeovers.

The Stock Market and Mergers in the United Kingdom

Hume Occasional Paper No.24 £7.50

A commissioned paper by E. Victor Morgan and Ann D. Morgan. Emeritus Professor and Mrs. Morgan are the authors, both individually and together, of numerous books and articles in various fields of economics.

After an introductory survey of the scope of the problem, including a discussion of the significance of corporate status and of current merger policy, the authors pose three questions.

1. Has the market proved to be a good discriminator between bids that are and those that are not in the public interest?

2. Does the market mechanism contain built-in bias towards either too much or too little merger activity?

3. Does market activity in relation to mergers produce significant 'side-effects'?

They offer the quick answers of Almost Certainly No, Probably Yes and Yes, before giving a description of the equity market which 'qualif(ies) the usual idea of the Stock Exchange as a market in which share prices are the outcome of a continuous trading process involving many bargains between a large number of traders actively competing with one another'. This may be true of the market in the top twenty or so companies but as the size of the companies diminishes so the number of transactions falls and elements of oligopoly appear. Research by market analysts is similarly concentrated on the top companies so that at the lower end of the market traders have to rely largely on information provided by the companies themselves.

The authors conducted a questionnaire survey of the sources of information used by institutional investors and their attitudes towards takeovers. They report their findings briefly in this paper and fully in Hume Occasional Paper No.25 (see below). They then analyse the market in the shares of a number of acquiring and target companies in the period 1st April 1989 to 31st March 1990 and find that this sector reflects the market as a whole: trading in the shares of a small number of large merging companies is active, but in very many cases it is 'sporadic, the volume of transactions is low and competition among market-makers is oligopolistic'.

There follows a description of the advisory services available to merging companies including merchant bankers, accountants, lawyers and public relations consultants; of the regulatory constraints imposed upon the markets by the Government and its agencies, by the City Code on Takeovers and Mergers and by the Stock Exchange Listing Requirements. The influence of the various professional bodies is seen as 'creat(ing) a bias towards too much rather than too little takeover activity'. The influence of the Government's current regulatory regime is seen as 'concentrated almost wholly on rather limited aspects of competition in the UK market; wider effects of mergers on the structure of the economy (being) almost wholly ignored ..... and making only trivial differences to the operation of the market'. The City Takeover Code, concerned almost exclusively with ensuring fair treatment of shareholders, especially those in target companies, is also seen as 'contribut(ing) to the bias towards merger activity that exists in the system as a whole'. The Stock Exchange Rules are seen as favouring takeovers of small companies by large ones whilst leaving very large firms with freedom to bid for 'an enormous range of possible targets ..... without encountering any significant obstacle from Stock Exchange Rules'.

The paper then provides an economic analysis of current mergers policy starting from the efficient market hypothesis and it reviews the empirical evidence in order to test the information-arbitrage-efficiency and the fundamental-valuation hypotheses. These technical sections are followed by a summary of the evidence and by comments on some effects of mergers on financial markets and on the economy as a whole.

Finally, under three heads, the authors offer suggestions of remedies for a situation which they describe as follows. 'The best that can be said for the present regime for mergers is that it leads to the spending of a lot of time and money for very little good; at worst, the results are positively harmful'.

1. *Removing bias* in favour of takeover activity by extending to a wider range of situations the Stock Exchange requirement that large companies obtain the approval of their shareholders in a general meeting to the making of bids, and by increasing the numbers of non-executive directors, who should give reasons why they believe a bid to be in their shareholders' interest. Bid documents should include information about the contracts and remuneration of professional advisors. The mandatory bid rules and constraints on defensive action in the City Takeover Code also discriminates in favour of takeovers and this tendency should be mitigated.

2. *The quality and use of information*, which affect share prices and hence the bids that are likely to be made, are matters to which the investment management industry should given attention, possibly by reducing duplication of research and by collective pressure 'to elicit more information about the logical basis for proposing or opposing mergers'.

3. *The regulatory framework* provided by the DTI, the OFT and the MMC, which 'suffers from an inadequate concept of competition and an almost total neglect

of externalities', could be improved by providing that 'mega-mergers' (above certain suggested thresholds or certain turnover criteria) should, subject to ministerial discretion, be referred automatically to the MMC.

Investment Managers and Takeovers: Information and Attitudes

Hume Occasional Paper No.25 £3.50

A commissioned paper by Emeritus Professor E. Victor Morgan and Ann D. Morgan which supplements their paper *The Stock Market and Mergers in the United Kingdom*, Hume Occasional Paper No.24, see above.

The paper opens with a description of the organisation of institutional asset management, an industry in which there has been much change in the last two decades, especially since the 'Big Bang' in 1986. Among the most significant changes have been the creation of 'financial conglomerates', the sale of financial management services on a fee-paying basis, the virtual disappearance of independent institutional brokers and the emergence of very large managed funds. The pressures on investment managers to secure high returns 'including those generated by takeovers and rumours of takeovers' are described.

As part of the research for their paper mentioned above, the authors conducted a questionnaire survey among investment managers to seek evidence on the sources and quality of the information available to institutional investment managers in relation to companies which may be involved in takeovers, and their opinions on its value. They also sought to test the assertion that institutions usually tend to support existing managements in takeover situations and to probe the attitudes of investment managers to such issues as 'short-termism'. The results of the survey are reported fully. The main findings may be summarised as follows.

The principal sources of information available to investment managers are in-house research and brokers' recommendations, and much less important, advice from other professional advisors and media comment. Most funds use a substantial number of brokers, different funds probably using the same brokers.

There are wide variations in the number of qualified staff by whom investment managers are supported.

A high proportion of investment managers regard takeover offer and defence documents as moderately useful but many were critical of the objectivity of these documents.

When asked about their initial attitude towards a bid, most respondents said that they considered each case on its merits but a substantial minority said that they supported existing management unless dissatisfied with its record.

A high proportion of respondents claimed that they 'often' or 'sometimes' opposed a bid, either informally or at a shareholders' meeting, or both.

Asked to rate the factors that might influence a decision to accept or reject a bid, the 'long-term prospects of the target' ranked highest, 'the long-term prospect of the bidder' ranked next and 'the immediate value of a bid', only third.

The authors' general conclusion is that 'a large majority of voting rights in British industrial and commercial companies is in the hands, not of those who ultimately gain or lose by these companies' performance, but of a group of professional managers whose reward comes in salaries and career prospects, not from shares in 'their' companies. The Government's observation that 'the people best placed to make a judgement of commercial prospects are those whose money is at stake' is almost wholly irrelevant here'.

Taxation and Mergers Policy

Hume Occasional Paper No.26 £2.00

Contributed by John Chown, a tax specialist with extensive experience of mergers and reorganisations, both domestic and international.

In his introduction, the author states that tax law and company law in the UK normally place no obstacles in the way of mergers between domestic companies; generally there are no adverse tax consequences either at shareholder or at company level. However, past tax anomalies have led to distortions of industrial structures which still persist. De-mergers, on the other hand, have been less leniently treated and despite some remedial legislation 'there is still no wholly satisfactory and generally available way in which unwieldy conglomerates, resulting from past merger frenzies, can, of their own initiative, break themselves up into more manageable component parts'. Cross border mergers are also beset with obstacles which make it difficult to create a company whose shareholders and activities are spread across the EC rather than concentrated in one country.

The paper continues with an analysis of four main types of tax distortion in the field of mergers.

1. *Bias against company distribution* of dividends in the 1965 system of Corporation Tax led companies with cash flows in excess of re-investment opportunities to make acquisitions of dubious industrial logic. The effect of this reluctance to distribute surplus cash to shareholders for their own re-investment 'distorted industrial decisions for a generation'.

2. *Bias against private companies* was caused by confiscatory personal tax rates alongside reasonable company tax rates. The penal taxation of 'close' companies in 1965 made it attractive to their owners to sell out to conglomerates. Although these penal provisions no longer apply, some of the conglomerates remain 'as a rag bag of unrelated businesses'.

3. *Bias against foreign earnings* was caused by the 1972 Corporation Tax reforms which, though designed to create a level playing field for dividends, introduced some distortions that still persist as obstacles to true Europe-wide mergers. The requirement to pay Advance Corporation Tax at the same time as a dividend payment is a substantial extra burden where dividends are paid out of foreign earnings rather than UK taxed profits. This led companies with international earnings to make acquisitions simply to acquire UK earnings. This distortion continues.

4. Tax losses and capital allowances were, until 1984, factors which induced 'fiscally starved' companies making heavy capital investments to merge with profitable but not capital intensive companies such as those in the retailing and financial services sectors. There were also mergers based on the use of tax losses and undertaken to take advantage of Capital Gains Tax losses.

The author concludes by providing seven short case studies to illustrate mergers induced by the tax factors which he has described.

Evidence Submitted to the Inquiry

Hume Occasional Paper No.27 £3.50

In Hume Occasional Paper No.18, see above, there were published five responses to an invitation made to individuals, organisations and to the public at large to make their views on corporate takeovers known to the Inquiry. This paper publishes three more responses.

The Scottish Office

This memorandum complements one by the DTI published in HOP No.18. It emphasises that there is only one competition policy in the UK endorsed by Ministers collectively. Thus there is no divergence of view on the structure of that policy. Nevertheless in individual cases it is possible for different Government departments to have different views about the application of that policy. A Merger Panel consisting of representatives of interested Government departments, including the Scottish Office, is available to enable the Director General of the OFT to obtain these departmental views in order to advise the Secretary of State for Trade and Industry on whether to make a reference to the MMC.

As a territorial department, the Scottish Office is likely to be aware of any regional considerations in cases involving Scottish companies. Such considerations, though subordinate to those of competition, are not excluded as reasons for reference to the MMC, and once a reference has been made, one of the specific aspects of a case that must be considered is 'the desirability .... of maintaining and promoting the balanced distribution of industry and employment in the UK'.

The position of Scottish Ministers on special protection for Scottish companies is stated as follows. 'They take the view that the economic health of the UK as a whole is secured by maintaining commercially diverse and dynamic regional economies. But they are equally clear that competition policy is not to be used as an arm of regional policy and that any sort of policy, formal or informal, of regional protectionism would be inconsistent with UK competition policy; would hinder the development of competition to the disadvantage of customer and consumer; and would ultimately be to the detriment of the health of business in Scotland'. But the avenue of a reference to the MMC on regional grounds has been kept open and 'The Scottish Office will continue to look at cases as they arise, and consider whether a proposed merger gives rise to legitimate regional concern'.

The University of Edinburgh Centre for Theology and Public Issues

The memorandum starts with an assertion that takeovers are of themselves neither good nor bad but that there are too many of the wrong sort. It then lists a series of concerns. Too many takeovers seem to be founded on a narrow view of a company as a mere vehicle for money-making rather than as a complex social and economic organism living in a community. The real owners, the shareholders, are largely passive and do not exercise the responsibilities that come with ownership. The threat of takeover tends to lead management to seek short-term success and to neglect long-term development. It seems increasingly uncertain that takeovers do in fact lead to a more efficient use of resources and many seem to be motivated less by industrial logic than by greed and empire-building. This latter tendency seems to be reinforced by the encouragement of professional advisors who thereby earn large fees. Takeovers lead to a centralisation of power and in some cases constitute an abuse of the right to compete in a free society.

There follows a statement of underlying convictions about the process of creating wealth which leads to a series of proposals for:

limitations on the rights of short-term or speculative shareholders;

new mechanisms for helping individual investors to exercise their responsibilities as shareholders;

changing the remit of fund managers to induce them to take broader views of their responsibilities;

more stringent Company Law to restrain excesses, and rules to make it easier to identify the ultimate beneficial owners of shares;

a wider remit for the OFT;

alternatives to takeover as a method of improving efficiency;

criteria for judging the legitimate takeover.

Mr. Dennis Henry

Mr. Henry's memorandum draws on a database of Scottish commercial and industrial companies which he established in his capacity as a management consultant.

First he analyses by size the companies the control of which went out of Scotland and lists some of the better known instances. He goes on to quantify the scale of the losses showing that the companies taken were capital-intensive rather than labour-intensive and that, judged by performance and rate of growth, they were also the better quality ones. As regards employment, job losses have not been large among the weekly-paid staff and junior management but have been significant among senior and high quality jobs. He then analyses the secondary impact on the providers of professional and other services, finding significant losses in the number and quality of jobs.

In a discussion of ways of avoiding takeover, he suggests that 'making the assets sweat' is the only effective self defence and goes on to show that, as Scottish companies are failing to meet national standards of performance, they remain vulnerable to acquisition.

He concludes that it is unlikely that in future there will be takeover activity on the scale seen in the two years 1985 and 1986, when companies in the commercial and industrial sector responsible for 53 per cent of the capital then employed were lost, if only for the reason that there are no longer sufficient large companies left in Scotland. He adds wryly that 'While we cannot put a ring fence around Scottish industry, it seems that our grouse, salmon and deer are more effectively protected from human predators than our industry'.

The Control of Mergers and Takeovers in the EC

Hume Occasional Paper No.29 £7.50

A commissioned paper by Robert Pringle who is a Director of the economics consultancy Graham Bannock and Partners Ltd. and a Senior Research Fellow of The David Hume Institute.

The paper opens with a statistical description of the unprecedented boom in takeover activity in the EC which started in the early 1980s and which continues. Its main causes are attributed to re-structuring due to heightened national and international competition, to the prospect of the Single European Market in 1992 which is itself a response to heightened international competition, to the ready availability of capital market finance for increased corporate borrowing and to the generally permissive merger policies of national governments. Takeover of companies in one member state of the EC by those in another member state is the fastest growing sector of this booming activity. However, '(b)ecause the legal framework for a European company does not yet exist, there cannot be a true 'fusion' of two partners in a company with a new legal personality transcending both of them', many EC mergers have much in common with traditional foreign direct investment aimed principally at securing market access and gaining 'information synergies'.

There follows a short survey of national mechanisms for controlling mergers which emphasises that existing differences are rooted in cultural traditions arising from differing patterns of ownership and social behaviour. Britain and Germany are the only countries having strong established machinery for controlling mergers.

The author then describes the main features of EC merger policy. He summarises the EC Mergers Regulation which came into force on 21st September 1990. It is designed to be the cornerstone of EC competition policy and to contribute to the successful completion of the Single European Market. Its purpose is to protect the competition process by preventing the acquisition of monopoly power. A merger will be deemed incompatible with the common market if it 'creates or strengthens a dominant position as a result of which competition would be significantly impeded.' There is, nevertheless, some scope in the interpretation of the Regulation for other 'public interest' issues to be considered and for defining the market for a product broadly or narrowly. He examines the working of the Regulation during its first six months. Jurisdictional problems have arisen relating to 'co-operative' or 'concentrative' joint ventures, to the definition of 'controlling interest' and the definition of 'a group' for the purpose of calculating the turnover criterion. But despite these technical problems, he reports general satisfaction with the way the Commission is operating the Regulation to monitor mergers with a European dimension through a 'one-stop shop.' Admittedly no difficult customers have yet appeared and, so far, there have been no conflicts with the various national regulatory shops, though these might arise if there were to be a spate of mega-mergers.

The author then turns to the other major aspect of the control of mergers, the development of rules of conduct to govern the behaviour of participants during the course of a takeover: a responsibility of a different (company law) Directorate of the Commission. Once again, deep cultural differences underly the difficulties in drafting a Directive which accommodates both the Continental preference for specific statutory regulation of commercial activity and the Anglo-Saxon preference for freedom and self-regulation. There is great anxiety that the adoption of a Directive based on the Continental approach will undermine the position of the UK Takeover Panel so that, instead of providing a speedy, flexible and certain system of self-regulation, it will become merely a stop on the way to the Courts to engage in tactical litigation, to the detriment of shareholders.

Drawing the threads of his analysis together in the concluding section, the author stresses the positive contribution which the merger control system has already made to the economic development of the EC but poses the question 'whether this whole apparatus of control will end up serving the interests of the European corporate state – companies and governments – rather than the individual consumer.' The answer will depend on whether merger policy is complemented by a wide range of other economic policies.

There are three important Appendices to the paper, a note on recent cases considered by the Commission, the text of the EC Merger Control Regulation and a note on The UK Takeover Panel and the draft 13th Company Law Directive.

Note: As the final texts of HOPs 30 and 31 were not available before this Report was sent to the publishers no summaries have been provided. The Institute hopes to publish these last two papers in May 1991.

Index